THE

OLD TIME
Hockey
TRIVIA

THE ORIGINAL SIX

OLD TIME Hockey TRIVIA

DON WEEKES

GREYSTONE BOOKS

Douglas & McIntyre
Vancouver/Toronto

For "The Flying Dinosaurs Line":
Paul Normand, Gerry Halton and Dave Fonda.

Copyright © 1995 by Don Weekes

95 96 97 98 99   5 4 3 2 1

Greystone Books
A division of Douglas & McIntyre Ltd.
1615 Venables Street
Vancouver, British Columbia V5L 2H1

Canadian Cataloguing in Publication Data

Weekes, Don.
  Old-time hockey trivia

  ISBN 1-55054-453-5

  1. National Hockey League—Miscellanea. 2. Hockey—Miscellanea. I. Title.
GV847.8.N3W43 1995   796.962'64   C95-910494-1

Editing by Kerry Banks and Anne Rose
Cover and text design by Peter Cocking
Front cover photograph courtesy of Imperial Oil–Turofsky/Hockey Hall of Fame
Back cover photograph courtesy of Dan Diamond & Associates, Inc.
Printed and bound in Canada by Best Book Manufacturers

Every reasonable care has been taken to trace the ownership of copyrighted visual material. Information that will enable the publishers to rectify any reference or credit is welcome.

The publisher gratefully acknowledges the assistance of the Canada Council and of the British Columbia Ministry of Tourism, Small Business and Culture.

Table of CONTENTS

THE WAY IT WAS

T HE ORIGINAL SIX ERA began in October 1942. World
War II was playing havoc with NHL rosters. Almost 80
NHLers had joined the armed forces, among them New
York's Colville brothers, Boston's entire Kraut Line, Kenny
Reardon of the Canadiens and Wally Stanowski of Toronto. The
best of the NHL's remaining forwards were the Bentley boys,
Lynn Patrick and Bryan Hextall. But there were others, such as
Maurice Richard and Ted Kennedy, both promising rookies,
who almost made fans forget that the NHL was in its fourth
wartime season. The calibre of play suffered; but never the box
office. Hockey became a morale booster for the home front.

(Answers are on page 7)

1.1 **What brought about the Original Six in 1942?**
A. World War II
B. The financial failure of an American NHL franchise
C. The addition of a new Canadian NHL franchise
D. The old Ottawa Senators

1.2 **Who beat Bobby Hull as rookie of the year in 1958?**
A. Stan Mikita
B. Ralph Backstrom
C. Tim Horton
D. Frank Mahovlich

1.3 **Which two Original Six goaltenders from the Maple Leafs had their No. 1 jerseys honoured in 1995?**
A. Johnny Bower and Terry Sawchuk
B. Johnny Bower and Frank McCool
C. Johnny Bower and Al Rollins
D. Johnny Bower and Turk Broda

1.4 **Who scored the most goals during the Original Six era?**
A. Bernie Geoffrion
B. Gordie Howe
C. Maurice Richard
D. Ted Lindsay

1.5 **To whom did Maurice Richard dedicate his 500th goal?**
A. His wife, Lucille
B. NHL president Clarence Campbell
C. Former Canadiens coach Dick Irvin
D. His father, Onésime Richard

1.6 **What significant event took place on October 5, 1965?**
A. Gordie Howe became the NHL's first 20-year player
B. Long-time NHL president Clarence Campbell retired
C. Mario Lemieux and Patrick Roy were born
D. The NHL announced league expansion plans for a second six-team division

1.7 **Who were the first brothers in NHL history to each lead the league in scoring?**
A. Gordie and Vic Howe
B. Lionel and Roy Conacher
C. Doug and Max Bentley
D. Maurice and Henri Richard

1.8 **Who invented the curved stick blade?**
A. An NHL player
B. An NHL executive
C. A hockey stick manufacturer
D. The 10-year-old son of a Stanley Cup-winning coach

1.9   **Who did Toronto trade to get Red Kelly in 1960?**
A. Howie Young
B. Marc Réaume
C. Marcel Pronovost
D. Hank Bassen

1.10   **What do Pete Babando, Bill Barilko, Elmer Lach, Tony Leswick and Henri Richard have in common?**
A. All registered shorthanded goals in overtime
B. Each played for Punch Imlach in junior hockey
C. All scored Stanley Cup-winning goals in overtime
D. All were inducted into the Hall of Fame just two years after retirement

1.11   **How many games did it take Gordie Howe to record 1,000 points?**
A. Less than 800 games
B. Between 800 and 900 games
C. Between 900 and 1,000 games
D. More than 1,000 games

1.12   **What famous forward line reunited in 1952 to play one more NHL game after a five-year retirement?**
A. The Kraut Line: Bauer–Schmidt–Dumart
B. The Kid Line: Jackson–Primeau–Conacher
C. The Punch Line: Blake–Lach–Richard
D. The Production Line: Lindsay–Abel–Howe

1.13   **Which Original Six goalie, after Terry Sawchuk, has the best shutout record?**
A. Glenn Hall
B. Al Rollins
C. Harry Lumley
D. Bill Durnan

1.14 **In 1953, managing director Frank Selke said: "All I did was open the Forum vault and say, 'Help yourself, Jean.'" How much money was, in fact, Jean Béliveau's first Montreal Canadiens contract worth? And for how long?**
A. Three years, $25,000, no signing bonus
B. Three years, $50,000, $5,000 signing bonus
C. Four years, $50,000, $10,000 signing bonus
D. Five years, $100,000, $20,000 signing bonus

1.15 **Who centred Gordie Howe and Ted Lindsay on Detroit's Production Line after Sid Abel retired in 1952?**
A. Earl Reibel
B. Norm Ullman
C. Glen Skov
D. Alex Delvecchio

1.16 **Name the last player to retire from the NHL who wore a Brooklyn Americans jersey. And what team was he playing for when he retired? (The Amerks folded in 1942.)**
A. Ken Mosdell
B. Harry Watson
C. Mel Hill
D. Pat Egan

1.17 **How many regular-season overtime games were played during the six-team era?**
A. Fewer than 10 games
B. An average of 12 games per season
C. An average of 24 games per season
D. An average of 36 games per season

1.18 **Which referee quit his NHL officiating job after being publicly criticized by league president Clarence Campbell?**
A. Frank Udvari
B. Red Storey
C. Eddie Powers
D. Bill Chadwick

1.19 **Name the only Original Six rookie to score five goals in one game.**
   A. Howie Meeker
   B. Bernie Geoffrion
   C. Ray Getliffe
   D. Bobby Rousseau

1.20 **Who centred for Bobby Hull when he set the NHL goal-scoring record of 54 goals in 1965–66?**
   A. Chico Maki
   B. Stan Mikita
   C. Phil Esposito
   D. Bill Hay

1.21 **Which Original Six Bruin played on three key forward lines for Boston during his career?**
   A. Don McKenney
   B. Johnny Bucyk
   C. Fleming Mackell
   D. Milt Schmidt

1.22 **Where did NHL players first seriously talk about forming a players' association?**
   A. At an annual golf tournament
   B. At an All-Star game
   C. At a hospital fund-raiser
   D. On a live radio broadcast

1.23 **Which Original Six sniper invented the slapshot?**
   A. Bernie Geoffrion
   B. Stan Mikita
   C. Phil Esposito
   D. Bobby Hull

1.24 **What was unusual about Boston's Jack Gelineau and his entry into the NHL?**
A. He won both the Calder Trophy as rookie of the year and the Hart Trophy as MVP
B. He was the first NHL goalie not to wear No. 1 on his jersey
C. He scored the winning goal in his first game
D. He was the first NHLer to come directly from collegiate ranks

1.25 **How many players, if any, recorded 100-point seasons during the six-term era?**
A. None
B. One player: Stan Mikita
C. Two players: Gordie Howe and Bobby Hull
D. Three players: Stan Mikita, Gordie Howe and Bobby Hull

1.26 **After Gordie Howe, which Original Six player spent the most seasons with the same team?**
A. Chicago's Stan Mikita
B. Detroit's Alex Delvecchio
C. Boston's Johnny Bucyk
D. Montreal's Henri Richard

1.27 **Who was the last Original Six player to skate in NHL action?**
A. Serge Savard
B. Carol Vadnais
C. Phil Esposito
D. Wayne Cashman

Answers

THE WAY IT WAS

1.1 **B. The financial failure of an American NHL franchise**
After 17 unremarkable seasons, the starred and striped New York/Brooklyn Americans ceased operations in 1942, reducing the NHL to a six-team operation. Fan support and newspaper coverage steadily dwindled for the Amerks, who competed in a sports-mad marketplace with their crosstown rivals, the Cup-winning Rangers, three major league baseball teams and numerous other champions in boxing and tennis.

1.2 **D. Frank Mahovlich**
Although Hull's rookie regular-season record (13–34–47 in 70 games) topped Mahovlich's (20–16–36 in 67 games), the Big M scored more points in Calder Trophy balloting than runner-up Hull. Mahovlich was teamed with Leaf linemates Ron Stewart and Dick Duff, two young veterans who complemented the St. Michael's College junior's long, powerful strides on the attack. From his first NHL season, Mahovlich demonstrated an uncanny scoring ability, with masterful stickhandling and dead-accurate shots. Mahovlich played in three decades with three NHL teams, repeatedly delivering what had been predicted from the beginning: that he was a smooth-skating playmaker with the Midas touch around the net.

1.3 **D. Johnny Bower and Turk Broda**
On March 11, 1995, the Maple Leafs hoisted two No. 1 sweaters into the Gardens' rafters in honour of Bower and Broda. Between them, the two had backstopped Toronto to eight Stanley Cups during the six-team era. (The ninth Cup came off the pads of Frank McCool.) Sawchuk wore the Leafs' No. 30.

Gordie Howe stickhandles against the Blackhawks.

1.4   **B. Gordie Howe**

From 1946–47 through 1966–67, Howe scored 649 goals in 1,398 regular-season games—a scoring average of .464 per game or 31 goals per season for 21 years!

The NHL's Top Ten Sharpshooters • 1942–1967

Goals	Player	Team(s)	Years
649	Gordie Howe	Detroit	1946–1967
544	Maurice Richard	Montreal	1942–1960
399	Jean Béliveau	Montreal	1950–1967
388	Bernie Geoffrion	Mtl/NYR	1950–1967*
379	Ted Lindsay	Det/Chi	1944–1965*
370	Bobby Hull	Chicago	1957–1967
328	Alex Delvecchio	Detroit	1950–1967
314	Andy Bathgate	NYR/Tor/Det	1952–1967
294	Norm Ullman	Detroit	1955–1967
281	Red Kelly	Det/Tor	1947–1967

* Includes retirement years.

1.5   **C. Former Canadiens coach Dick Irvin**

At the start of the 1943–44 season, Irvin predicted Richard would be "the biggest star in hockey." Sure enough, the Rocket proved Irvin right, but the coach never saw his superstar score the NHL's first 500th regular-season goal. Only months before Richard's big night of October 19, 1957, Irvin died. He had coached the Rocket for 13 seasons. In his honour, Richard dedicated his 500th to Irwin, because "I owed him a lot."

1.6   **C. Mario Lemieux and Patrick Roy were born**

Were the planetary axes aligned in vertical positions resembling goal posts to deliver this cosmic hockey "ka-pow," or what? The big bang happened on October 5, 1965, when two of hockey's future stars were born: Roy in Quebec City and Lemieux in Montreal.

Doug and Max Bentley after Max's trade to Toronto in 1947.

1.7   **C. Doug and Max Bentley**

The Bentleys came from Delisle, Saskatchewan. Despite a four-year age difference, they had remarkably similar NHL careers, entering the league in consecutive seasons beginning in 1939. Doug and kid brother Max each won the NHL scoring race at age 26, while they were both in their fourth NHL season, and with the same team, the Blackhawks. Doug's championship season came in 1942–43 (73 pts.); Max followed in 1945–46 (61 pts.) and 1946–47 (72 pts.). They played until 1953–54, when each brother hung up his blades with the Rangers. They were only one point apart in career totals: Doug had 543 points and Max 544. Naturally, both Bentleys are members of the Hockey Hall of Fame.

1.8   **A. An NHL player**
Most often credited with the curved stick are three players, Andy Bathgate, Stan Mikita and Bobby Hull, who in the late 1950s began experimenting with bent blades and the weird flight patterns they produced when firing a puck. Quite accidentally, Mikita began blasting shots with a broken bent blade during practice, and discovered its effectiveness on velocity and accuracy. (He then shared his discovery with Hull.) Meanwhile, Bathgate was trying similar stunts in New York. All three deserve credit for an innovation that changed hockey forever.

1.9   **B. Marc Réaume**
This ranks as the worst NHL one-for-one trade ever. Wings manager Jack Adams, believing Kelly was washed up, traded the veteran All-Star defenseman for Réaume, a low-impact Toronto rearguard. In the next seven seasons, Kelly, who was moved from blueline to forward, helped lead the Maple Leafs to four Stanley Cups, the last in 1967. Réaume managed just five points in 77 NHL games.

1.10   **C. All scored Stanley Cup-winning goals in overtime**
During the six-team era, five players won the Cup on sudden-death overtime goals, four coming in a five-year span between 1950 and 1954, and the fifth in 1966. Highlight: Detroit won two championships, in 1950 and 1954, on goals in seventh game extra-periods.

Seventh Game Overtime Stanley Cup-Winning Goals

Year	Cup-Winning Scorer	Winning Team	Losing Goalie	Game No.	Time/OT Cup Winner
1950	P. Babando	Detroit	C. Rayner	7th	28:31
1951	B. Barilko	Toronto	G. McNeil	5th	2:53
1953	E. Lach	Montreal	J. Henry	5th	1:22
1954	T. Leswick	Detroit	G. McNeil	7th	4:29
1966	H. Richard	Montreal	R. Crozier	6th	2:20

1.11 **C. Between 900 and 1,000 games**
Howe scored his 1,000th point (an assist) on November 27, 1960, while playing in his 15th season and 938th regular-season game.

1.12 **A. The Kraut Line: Bauer–Schmidt–Dumart**
Between 1937 and 1947 the Kraut Line became one of hockey's most explosive forward units, finishing 1-2-3 in the NHL's 1939–40 scoring race, and twice leading the Bruins to Stanley Cups (in 1939 and 1941). Bauer, Schmidt and Dumart came from Kitchener, Ontario, where they played junior together. When war broke out in Europe, the three served in Canada's Armed Forces. The line played two more years before Bauer retired in 1947, and again in one last game on March 18, 1952—five years after the goal scoring ended. "Da gahdan" was honouring Schmidt and Dumart, so for the occasion Bauer suited up with his former linemates. The magic that had won scoring championships returned and the colourful trio again demonstrated its special brand of playmaking. Assisted by Bauer and Dumart, Schmidt scored his 200th career goal; Bauer later potted a backhander past Chicago's Harry Lumley. It was a hero's homecoming, and the drama, played out before 13,909 appreciative fans, could not have been better scripted.

1.13 **C. Harry Lumley**
Second in shutouts only to Sawchuk during the six-team era, Lumley accumulated 71 SOs in his 16-year NHL career. He was among the game's best goalkeepers and won the Vezina Trophy with Toronto in 1953–54, the year he notched 13 shutouts and the only season he out-zeroed the great Sawchuk.

1.14 **D. Five years, $100,000, $20,000 signing bonus**
Selke's quote to the press at Béliveau's contract signing, about opening "the Forum vault," was literally true. For two years Selke tried to woo Béliveau away from the Quebec Senior League, but it wasn't until the Canadiens

bought the entire league and turned it professional that Le Gros Bill jumped to the big club. Under tremendous pressure to sign the province's second most popular player (after Rocket Richard), Selke offered Béliveau whatever he wanted. In 1953, $100,000 was a lot of cash, but the rookie was worth every penny. Overnight, Béliveau developed into the star player the Canadiens imagined he would, and one of the league's highest-paid players.

1.15 D. Alex Delvecchio

One minute you're a 20-year-old slogging it through America's industrial grimeland on the junior circuit, and the next you're centring one of hockey's biggest power lines, partnered with Gordie Howe and Ted Lindsay during Detroit's reign of championships. That was the heady reality Delvecchio woke up to in 1952, after Sid Abel retired and left the Wings without a centre for the Production Line. Manager Jack Adams figured Delvecchio's pinpoint passing and lightning-fast skating skills would prove the perfect complement for the famed Detroit wingers. Adams nailed it right. The following season, 1952–53, Delvecchio finished fifth in league scoring, and was named centre on the second All-Star team. He dominated offensively during the 1954 and 1955 Stanley Cups and played faithfully for the Wings until 1974. (Ullman also played with Howe and Lindsay, starting in 1957.)

1.16 A. Ken Mosdell

Despite the financial problems that cost the Americans their Brooklyn franchise, their last NHL team featured a few shining examples of what the future might have held had the club not folded. Mosdell, after his rookie year with the Amerks, packed for Montreal and Chicago where he played 14 seasons and starred on the league's second All-Star team in 1953–54. His last year was as a Canadien in 1957–58. Mosdell played one year longer than Watson, who retired in 1956–57. Egan hung up the blades in 1951, and Hill in 1946.

1.17 **A. Fewer than 10 games**

On November 21, 1942, the league cancelled overtime play in the regular season due to wartime restrictions on train scheduling. Since the league waited until 1983–84 to reinstate regular-season overtime, the only overtime games played by Original Six teams during the regular season occurred before the league pulled the plug on extra periods in the fall of 1942. So, who scored the only regular-season overtime winners during the six-team era?

Six-Team Era Regular-Season Overtimes

Date	Scores	Game Winners	OT Time
Nov. 7/42	New York 4 – Montreal 3	Alf Pike	4:22
Nov. 8/42	Chicago 3 – Detroit 3	*	
Nov. 10/42	New York 5 – Chicago 3	Bryan Hextall	1:02
		Lynn Patrick	7:11

*Overtime lasted a full 10 minutes without sudden-death provisions—teams scored as often as possible within that time or, if no goals resulted, the game ended in a draw.

1.18 **B. Red Storey**

Storey's resignation as an NHL referee was front page news in 1959. After being criticized by Campbell for "freezing" on an alleged trip by Montreal's Junior Langlois on Bobby Hull, Storey whistled the public denunciation as unfair and resigned, firing back: "When your decisions are not backed up by your boss, it's time to quit." According to Storey, Langlois hit Hull with a "beautiful hip check." The hometown Chicago crowd, smarting from an earlier non-call that resulted in a Montreal goal (during this very important playoff game), descended on Storey in a rage, throwing beer in his face and littering the ice with debris. The game was delayed for 25 minutes, and at one point the Canadiens' Doug Harvey had to rescue Storey after fans jumped him from behind. Montreal won the game (and the series), while Storey had to fight his way to the dressing room, fending off attacking fans with a borrowed stick. Campbell, who later regretted his "chat" with the press, claimed some of his comments had been taken out of context.

1.19   A. Howie Meeker

Six players between 1942 and 1967 celebrated five-goal games, including Getliffe, Geoffrion, Rousseau, Meeker, Maurice Richard and Syd Howe. But the only rookie among them was Howie, who shell-shocked Chicago's Paul Bibeault with the 12th, 13th, 14th, 15th and 16th goals of his career. The Maple Leaf rookie won the Calder Trophy, tallying a 27–18–45 record in 55 games.

1.20   C. Phil Esposito

Hull's so-called "Million-Dollar Line" (with Bill Hay and Murray Balfour) was tinkered with during its five-year term, but the big change came in 1965 when Esposito replaced Hay at centre. It was Espo's third NHL season (the second-to-last year before his Boston trade), and centring for Hull proved a winning move; Esposito scored 53 points (27G, 26A) to help Hull establish the 54-goal record.

1.21   B. Johnny Bucyk

Regarded by long-time Bruins manager Harry Sinden "as one of the best passing forwards of all time," Bucyk played 21 seasons in Boston, first on the Uke Line with Bronco Horvath and Vic Stasiuk, then on the B-O-W Line opposite Murray Oliver and Tommy Williams, and, finally, with Johnny McKenzie and Fred Stanfield during the 1970 and 1972 Stanley Cup years.

1.22   B. At an All-Star game

The first time players got together to discuss the idea of a player's association was at the 1956 NHL All-Star game in Montreal. Spearheaded by Detroit's Ted Lindsay and Montreal's Doug Harvey, a meeting was held after the match that included Jim Thomson of Toronto, Gus

Mortson of Chicago, Fernie Flaman of Boston and the Rangers' Bill Gadsby. The following day, each player returned to his respective club and began soliciting support. On February 11, 1957, the first NHL Players' Association was founded and immediately drew fire from team owners and league bosses. Under pressure, the union survived just one year, as defections among the membership soon eroded solidarity.

1.23 A. Bernie Geoffrion
Geoffrion never shied from making noise. His fierce temper and loud opinions often got him into referee trouble, but that wasn't what earned him the nickname "Boom-Boom" in the 1950s. At practice one day, reporters remarked on the thundering noise of his shots as they banged off the boards. The description personified the player and his explosive shots, which became harder and more accurate as he practised his unique wind-up. The Boomer was inventing the slapshot, the novel shooting technique that soon became standard weaponry in the sniper's scoring arsenal.

1.24 D. He was the first NHLer to come directly from collegiate ranks
Gelineau moved straight from the college hockey circuit as a McGill University goaltender to Boston in 1949–50. Although the Bruins finished in an unimpressive fifth place (22–32–16), Gelineau's performance (3.28 GAA) earned him the Calder Trophy as best rookie. His inspired play continued for another season (2.81 GAA), but after his trade to Chicago in 1953 Gelineau packed it in, soon forgotten except in trivia lore.

1.25 A. None
The first 100-point season was in 1968–69, two years after the six-team era. Mikita, Hull, Moore, Geoffrion and Howe all came within a whisker (97, 97, 96, 95 and 95 respectively) before league expansion in 1967, but not

until Phil Esposito's 100th on March 2, 1969, could the NHL celebrate the first 100-point player.

1.26   B. Detroit's Alex Delvecchio

The Red Wings' number two ironman, Delvecchio played 1,549 games in 24 NHL seasons with Detroit. Incredibly, he missed just 43 matches from 1951 through 1973 in a 22-season stretch, including seven consecutive seasons of uninterrupted hockey. Delvecchio ranks second to Gordie, not only in games played with one team, but also on the NHL's all-time games played list. Boston's Bucyk played 1,436 games in 21 years, Mikita 1,394 games in 22 Chicago seasons and Richard 1,256 contests in 20 years with the Canadiens.

1.27   D. Wayne Cashman

A 17-year Bruin, Cashman outdistanced Vadnais and Savard as the last player from the six-team era to see action by mere playoff games alone. Each began their careers prior to league expansion in 1967 and retired in 1982–83. Vadnais's career ended in the regular season when New Jersey failed to make the playoffs; Savard's career concluded after three 1983 playoff games with Winnipeg; Cashman's career finished in the 1983 Conference finals after eight post-season games. Esposito quit in 1980–81.

THE PINWHEEL PUCK

In this pinwheel game each word joins in the same way as a regular crossword. Starting at square No. 1, work clockwise around the four concentric rings or towards the centre along the spokes, filling in the right answer from the clues below. Each answer begins with the last letter of the previous word. Determine word length by using the clue numbers. (The answer to No. 1 is five letters long since the next clue is No. 3.)

(Solutions are on page 130)

Around

1. Babe _____
3. Toronto (abbr.)
4. Art _____
6. " _____ Jim" Henry
7. New York's Don _____
9. Mel _____
10. Rangers tough guy (full name)
13. Bobby _____
14. Dressing _____
15. New York arena (abbr.)
16. Hand equipment
18. Chicago's "_____ Line"
20. Jump
22. Many players pushed together
24. Play rule _____
25. Detroit's Alex _____
26. The Canadiens' Bert _____
27. Goalie Bill _____
28. Chicago's Eric _____
29. Mad or _____
30. Leading scorer in 1953 playoffs: Boston player (full name)
32. Canada and U.S.: two _____
34. She _____ the national anthem (past tense)
35. Maple Leaf _____
36. Goalie Don _____
37. _____ Abel
38. _____ Moore
39. Time ends
40. Deserve or _____
41. Offensive move up ice
42. _____-butt
43. _____ Clapper
44. Close or _____ scoring race
45. Even score
46. Life's future or _____
47. 12 months

Towards Centre

2. _____ Blake (3 letters)
5. Preserve or _____ a win
7. Rocket _____
8. New York's Rod _____
11. Skating space between players
12. Result of game
13. Shooters _____- _____-it into net
15. America's Olympic "_____ on Ice"
17. Bad or _____ temper (7 letters)
19. Standing _____
21. Muscle rubdown
23. The Leafs' Dickie _____ (4 letters)
31. Season record (opp. of wins)
33. Oxygen

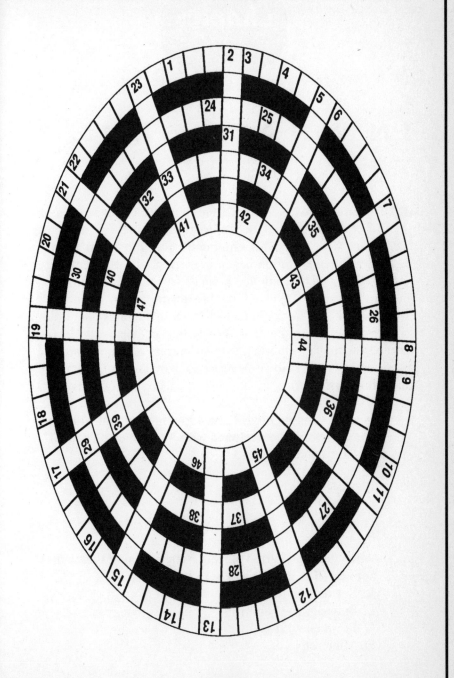

IN WHAT YEAR...?

T HE ERA KNOWN AS THE Golden Age of hockey shook off the conventions of the past and launched the game up-ice with new rules, equipment and, most importantly, new stars. The revolution began in earnest with the centre-ice redline, followed by a simple fibreglass face protector and, later, an American gold-medal Olympic team, which announced to the world that not only Canadians and Russians could play this ice game. From the dank, sweaty hockey palaces of the old NHL, a new hockey emerged with spectators who now watched stars such as Gordie Howe, Maurice Richard and Bobby Hull on televison "sets." *(Answers are on page 23)*

2.1 **In what year did the NHL hold its first "annual" All-Star game? (Not to be confused with Ace Bailey's "benefit" All-Star game in 1934.)**

A. 1937
B. 1942
C. 1947
D. 1952

2.2 **When were penalized players from opposing teams first separated in the penalty box?**

A. Between 1950 and 1955
B. Between 1956 and 1960
C. Between 1961 and 1965
D. After 1965

2.3 **In what year did Gordie Howe overtake Maurice Richard's NHL scoring record of 544 goals? (Hint: Richard retired in 1960.)**
A. 1961–62
B. 1963–64
C. 1965–66
D. 1967–68

2.4 **In what season did Jacques Plante first wear his mask in an NHL game?**
A. 1956–57
B. 1957–58
C. 1958–59
D. 1959–60

2.5 **In what year did the United States win its first Olympic gold medal in hockey?**
A. 1952
B. 1956
C. 1960
D. 1964

2.6 **In what season did Terry Sawchuk break the NHL's career shutout record of 94 SOs, set by George Hainsworth in 1936?**
A. 1960–61
B. 1963–64
C. 1966–67
D. 1969–70

2.7 **In what year did George Armstrong, Glenn Hall, Jean Béliveau, Andy Bathgate and Gordie Howe (the first time) retire?**
A. 1970
B. 1971
C. 1972
D. 1973

2.8 **In what year did the first black player join the NHL?**
A. 1948
B. 1953
C. 1958
D. 1963

2.9 **In what year did the NHL require all teams to carry an "extra" goalie on the bench during game play?**
A. 1950
B. 1955
C. 1960
D. 1965

2.10 **In what season did Maurice Richard score 50 goals in 50 games?**
A. 1944–45
B. 1946–47
C. 1948–49
D. 1950–51

2.11 **In what year was the centre redline introduced?**
A. 1943–44
B. 1945–46
C. 1947–48
D. 1949–50

2.12 **In which decade did Gordie Howe record his best single-season point total?**
A. The 1940s
B. The 1950s
C. The 1960s
D. The 1970s

2.13 **In what season did the NHL require all arenas to paint their ice surfaces white?**
A. 1944–45
B. 1949–50
C. 1954–55
D. 1959–60

IN WHAT YEAR...?

2.1 **C. 1947**
While the league had been organizing benefit All-Star matches and selecting first and second All-Star teams since 1930, the first official All-Star game was held in the fall of 1947. Playing for the All-Stars were Turk Broda, Bill Quackenbush, Jack Stewart, Maurice Richard and Ted Lindsay. They defeated the Stanley Cup champion Maple Leafs 4–3, with proceeds donated to the players' pension fund.

2.2 **C. Between 1961 and 1965**
Maple Leaf Gardens was the first NHL arena to provide separate penalty boxes for home and visiting teams, beginning in November 1963. Construction began after an on-ice fight between the Leafs' Bob Pulford and the Canadiens' Terry Harper carried over into the Maple Leaf Gardens' "shared" box. Neither the first nor last sin-bin fight, it delivered an early knockout punch to end the problem.

2.3 **B. 1963–64**
Howe broke Richard's record to become the NHL's new all-time scoring leader on November 10, 1963. Two weeks earlier, Howe had tied the Rocket's career mark of 544 goals, but suddenly slumped. Then, at the Olympia, against Richard's former team, the Canadiens, Howe unleashed a howitzer from 25 feet that picked the inside corner to beat Charlie Hodge. After the match, the Canadiens showed class as Jean Béliveau presented the Red Wing star with a portrait of himself to celebrate the occasion.

Jacques Plante and the future face of goaltending.

2.4   **D. 1959–60**
Perhaps the greatest shots Plante faced in his magnificent
and unusual career came from critics (managers, coaches
and even fellow goalies) who targeted him as a rebel and
coward for his facemask. Plante challenged everyone,
stepping into the direct line of fire at Madison Square
Garden on November 1, 1959, after a blistering Andy
Bathgate backhand turned his nose into pulp. Plante
retreated to the medical clinic, bloodied but not intimidated. The four-time Vezina Trophy winner pulled out
his self-styled mask and stood up to coach Toe Blake and
the other skeptics. Blake reluctantly agreed to allow the
mask, and Plante put a new face on the future of goaltending. Final score: Canadiens 3–1 over New York.

2.5   **C. 1960**
The first time America won the Olympic gold medal in
ice hockey was at the 1960 Winter Olympic Games in
Squaw Valley, California. Leading the way for Uncle Sam
were goalie Jack McCartan, the Christian brothers and
Tommy Williams (who would later go on to an NHL
career). Like the "Miracle on Ice" team of the 1980
Olympic Games in Lake Placid, New York, this was
America's moment of glory and a sweet victory for an
underrated team. They stunned the hockey world, com-
piling a perfect record, 7–0–0, to upset the favoured
Canadians (silver) and the Soviets (bronze).

2.6   **B. 1963–64**
Sawchuk smashed Hainsworth's SO record on January 18,
1964, logging his 95th shutout in a 2–0 win over
Hainsworth's former team, the Canadiens. Hainsworth
set the record during 11 seasons and 465 games, Sawchuk
equalled the mark during his 15th season after 783 games.

2.7   **B. 1971**
The careers of five of the best Original Six players concluded after the 1970–71 season. Each veteran played at
least 17 years and entered the Hall of Fame.

2.8 **C. 1958**

Willie O'Ree became the first black player in NHL history on January 18, 1958. A native of Fredericton, New Brunswick, O'Ree made his NHL debut with the Bruins, playing only two matches before returning to the minors, but coming back again in 1960–61 to score four goals and 10 assists in 43 games. He was frequently the target of racial abuse, not only from opposing players, who goaded him with slurs, but from fans who threw black hats onto the ice to taunt him. O'Ree retired in 1980. In 25 pro years, it's said he never made more than $17,000 per season.

2.9 **D. 1965**

Although many teams already had two goalies—a regular starter and a spare for practice—it was not until the 1965 playoffs that the NHL mandated all clubs to have a net-minder on the bench, dressed to play. Before the rule change, home teams would provide a spare if either club sustained an injury to their starter. The spares, usually amateur and practice goalies or club trainers, sat in the stands and only dressed when needed, delaying games for long stretches. That tradition, and the split-second careers of transient replacements such as Detroit trainer Lefty Wilson, ended with the two-goalie sytem.

2.10 **A. 1944–45**

Assisted by linemates Elmer Lach and Toe Blake, Richard set a wicked pace in 1944–45 to score 50-in-50. But his momentous feat was anything but assured. In fact, the Rocket pocketed number 50 in the final match of the 50-game schedule—with just 2:15 remaining on the clock!

2.11 **A. 1943–44**

The Rangers' Frank Boucher and men like Art Ross of Boston and Hap Day of Toronto revolutionized the game when they introduced the centre redline to hockey in 1943–44. The line sped up play, enabling players to pass the puck from their own zone to centre ice. It also reduced offside infractions and the grinding style of play that was so common under the old rules, which forced players to carry the puck over the bluelines. While at one time strong forechecking teams could hem opponents in their zone for long periods, the new rules gave defenders greater mobility to counterattack through speed and passing. The offensive potential proved potent in 1943–44, when four teams surpassed the 200-goal mark, an NHL first.

2.12 **C. The 1960s**
Although Howe was a six-time NHL scoring champion during the six-team era, he managed to exceed his own personal offensive records with a 103-point season in 1968–69—at age 40. Yes, Howe's best season happened after expansion against weaker teams, but only two players scored more that season: young fellas Phil Esposito (126) and Bobby Hull (107). Other veterans, such as Jean Béliveau, Frank Mahovlich and Stan Mikita, fell behind. Howe's highest single-season point total during the six-team era was 95 points in 1952–53.

2.13 **B. 1949–50**
Prior to 1948, ice surfaces around the league were not tinted or painted, but had a drab grey look that came from the arenas' concrete floors. As the game wore on, the ice deteriorated with snow and scratches, which made the puck harder to follow, especially after the advent of television.

THE RECORD HOLDERS

Gordie Howe, Maurice Richard and Bobby Hull may dominate the record books of the six-team era, but they are not the only record holders. Match the players listed below with the Original Six records they achieved. (In brackets are the number of goals, points, shutouts, etc., that set the mark.)

(Solutions are on page 131)

Jean Béliveau	Bobby Hull	Jerry Toppazzini
Stan Mikita	Terry Sawchuk	Bernie Geoffrion
Gus Bodnar	Andy Bathgate	Maurice Richard
Gordie Howe	Harry Lumley	Syd Howe
Glenn Hall	Howie Meeker	Bill Durnan

1._____ Most Goals/One Season (54)

2._____ Most Assists/One Season (62)

3._____ Longest Goal Streak/One Season (10)

4._____ Most Shutouts/One Season by a Rookie (12)

5._____ Most Hat Tricks (26)

6._____ Most Consecutive +40-Goal Seasons (3)

7._____ Most Shorthanded Goals/One Season (7)

8._____ Longest SO Sequence by Goalie (309:21)

9._____ Most Goals/One Season by a Rookie (30)

10._____ Most Wins/One Season by a Goalie (44)

11._____ Most Goals/One Game (6)

12._____ Most Points/One Season by a Rookie (62)

13._____ Longest Assist Streak/One Season (11)

14._____ Most Shutouts/One Season (13)

15._____ Most Goals/One Game by a Rookie (5)

Chapter THREE

THE D-MEN

DURING THE SIX-TEAM ERA, the defenseman's primary role was to take care of his own end. Traditional rearguards, such as Allan Stanley, Leo Boivin and Butch Bouchard, plied their trade with heavy hits and solid backchecking, which produced some of the most competitive low-scoring games in the history of hockey. But there was another small group of intrepid blueliners, whose skills surpassed the standard defensive positional play of their contemporaries. They could control the tempo and flow of the game, lead a headlong rush through traffic or deliver pinpoint passing right on the tape. If Bobby Orr changed hockey by revolutionizing his position, he did it in the tradition of maverick D-men such as Doug Harvey, Pierre Pilote and Tim Horton. *(Answers on page 32)*

3.1 **Who was the first defenseman in NHL history to score 20 goals in a season?**
A. Doug Mohns
B. Frank "Flash" Hollett
C. Pat Egan
D. Red Kelly (as a Red Wing)

3.2 **What was the greatest number of goals Doug Harvey ever scored in one season?**
A. Under five goals
B. Between five and 10 goals
C. Between 11 and 15 goals
D. Between 16 and 20 goals

3.3 Who was the first NHL defenseman to play a full season without registering a penalty? (Hint: He was the first rearguard to win the Lady Byng Trophy.)
A. Doug Harvey
B. Jacques Laperriere
C. Tim Horton
D. Bill Quackenbush

3.4 Which Original Six defenseman holds the NHL record for most regular-season appearances without winning the Stanley Cup?
A. Harry Howell
B. Allan Stanley
C. Doug Mohns
D. Bill Gadsby

3.5 Who was the only defenseman to become a leading playoff scorer during the six-team era?
A. Bobby Orr
B. Tim Horton
C. Pierre Pilote
D. Allan Stanley

3.6 Which Maple Leaf defenseman scored a crucial game-winner on a broken ankle in the 1964 playoffs?
A. Bobby Baun
B. Allan Stanley
C. Carl Brewer
D. Tim Horton

3.7 Which defenseman scored Toronto's 1951 Stanley Cup-winning goal?
A. Jim Thomson
B. Bill Barilko
C. Gus Mortson
D. Bill Juzda

3.8 Who holds the Original Six record for most points scored by a rearguard in one playoff year?
A. Leo Boivin
B. Red Kelly (as a Red Wing)
C. Tim Horton
D. Jacques Laperriere

3.9 Who was the only defenseman to win the Hart Trophy as league MVP during the six-team era?
A. Babe Pratt
B. Red Kelly
C. Doug Harvey
D. Tim Horton

3.10 Who was the last defenseman to win the Norris Trophy before Bobby Orr took control for an unprecedented eight seasons?
A. Harry Howell
B. Tim Horton
C. Jacques Laperriere
D. Pierre Pilote

3.11 Who was the last defenseman to win the Lady Byng Trophy as the league's most gentlemanly player?
A. Bill Quackenbush
B. Doug Harvey
C. Jacques Laperriere
D. Red Kelly (as a Red Wing)

3.12 Which Original Six defenseman captured the Norris Trophy as the league's top rearguard, while coaching an NHL team?
A. Carl Brewer
B. Doug Harvey
C. Bill Gadsby
D. Tom Johnson

T H E   D - M E N

3.1 **B. Frank "Flash" Hollett**
They called him "Flash" because under the tutelage of
Boston's Eddie Shore and Dit Clapper, Hollett became
one of early hockey's great rushing defensemen. His
adeptness at stickhandling and setting up scoring plays
on the rush proved invaluable to the Bruins during
their Stanley Cup campaigns of 1939 and 1941. Despite
recording two 19-goal seasons for Boston, manager Art
Ross unwisely traded Hollett to Detroit, where Flash
again performed All-Star manoeuvres on the blueline,
finally notching the first 20-goal season (1944–45) by a
defenseman. Hollett's record stood until Bobby Orr's 21
goals in 1968–69.

3.2 **B. Between five and 10 goals**
Doug Harvey was one of hockey's greatest D-men,
although in a career that included 19 NHL seasons, seven
Norris Trophies as outstanding defenseman, 13 All-Star
appearances and six Stanley Cups, he never scored more
than nine goals in a season. But when it came to controlling a game, Harvey was peerless. Rarely did he direct an
errant pass or rush a play without his winger in position.
He used to say, sarcastically, that he didn't score because
there were no bonuses in his contract for goals. Still,
Harvey wasn't the stay-at-home low-scoring rearguard
typical of his era; his offensive style was the forerunner to
Bobby Orr's. Harvey could kill time on a penalty or lead a
rush up-ice with equal deftness, manoeuvring in and out
almost effortlessly among forecheckers to deliver a soft
pass to Canadiens forwards before returning to defend
the blueline. Harvey scored only 88 goals but assisted on
452 in 1,113 games.

Controlling the play. **Doug Harvey** wastes another victim.

3.3 D. Bill Quackenbush

It's not surprising that Quackenbush became the NHL's first Lady Byng winner (most gentlemanly player) from the defense corps. The position demands the sublime discipline of stealing the puck from an attacker and Quackenbush did this more effectively than anyone else in the six-team era, checking players without holding or tripping and stopping a rush cold without boarding. His low penalty totals are indicative of his clean style of play, which never betrayed the Hall-of-Famer in 14 NHL seasons. In that time, Quackenbush accumulated just 95 career penalty minutes (0.12 minutes per game) and earned the honour of being hockey's first rearguard to play a penalty-free season (in 1948–49). But his longevity had as much to do with his airtight defense as with his offensive skills, which often equalled those of the great Doug Harvey for puck control, or Red Kelly's talent for playmaking.

3.4 A. Harry Howell

Howell's 1,411 games in 21 seasons ranks fifth among all-time games-played, but first among Cup-less NHLers. Bluelining for New York, California and Los Angeles between 1952 and 1973, Howell didn't even get to the Stanley Cup finals, nor did he play on a first-place team.

3.5 C. Pierre Pilote

Pilote should be classed with the Orrs, Robinsons and MacInnises in the playoff record books, given that he was the only Original Six defenseman to earn top points in a post-season scoring race. He would win the Norris Trophy as top rearguard on three successive occasions and play in eight All-Star games, but perhaps Pilote's greatest achievement came mid-career in Chicago's breakthrough playoff year of 1961. The Hawks D-man led the rush and worked the corners, besting Chicago's offensive gunners, Bobby Hull and Stan Mikita, to tie Gordie Howe as playoff scoring leader and record 15 points. It was Chicago's last Cup to date; Pilote was named the Blackhawk's captain the following season.

Pierre Pilote, one of hockey's best rushing rearguards, charges by Montreal's Henri Richard.

3.6   **A. Bobby Baun**

In the annals of playoff hockey, the story of Baun's sixth-game 1964 overtime winner is a testament to courage. With the score tied 3–3 and Toronto facing elimination, Baun takes a Gordie Howe slapper off the ankle. Carried away on a stretcher, the worst is expected. In overtime, out skates Baun on a frozen and taped ankle, and at the 2:43 mark lobs a shot that bounces past a maze of players and beyond a confused Terry Sawchuk. Baun's sudden-death goal propels the Leafs into game seven. Baun goes into the finale on crutches, but plays without missing a shift as Toronto whips Detroit 4–0 to win another Stanley Cup. The next day, doctors examined Baun and confirmed what he already suspected: a broken ankle.

3.7   **B. Bill Barilko**

Known as "Bashing Bill" for his punishing body checks, Barilko was a member of Conn Smythe's rugged defensive corps, which dominated the game for five years and propelled Toronto to four Stanley Cups between 1947 and 1951. Barilko's Cup-winning goal in 1951 is probably Toronto's best remembered, not just for the heroic manner in which he scored it, but for the tragedy that followed. During overtime of game five of the Cup finals against Montreal, Barilko charged in from the blueline and fired a puck from the face-off circle at Montreal's Gerry McNeil. Barilko's windup was delivered with such momentum, he fell forward as the shot gunned past McNeil to win the Cup. The Leafs were champions and Barilko the hero. But he would never play again. That summer, on a fishing trip to northern Ontario, his plane went down and vanished without a trace. Ominously, it marked the end of a championship era for the Leafs. Barilko's body was later found, but not until June 7, 1963, just weeks after Toronto captured the Stanley Cup—only its second since the plane crash.

3.8   C. Tim Horton

Despite what Punch Imlach or any other NHL coach demanded of Horton, he always played the game his way. Although he listened to advice, picking from it what he could use, Horton remained true to his own hockey sense, developing skills that went far beyond the one-dimensional defensive game he was taught. His independence challenged some, but made him one of the league's most explosive rushing rearguards. During the 1962 Stanley Cup finals, Horton established the defenseman's record in playoff scoring, amassing 16 points (3 goals, 13 assists) in 12 games. His biggest point came against Chicago on Dick Duff's Cup-winning goal, a result of one of the classic end-to-end rushes that made him a dominant player of the great Leaf teams of the 1960s.

3.9   A. Babe Pratt

Unofficially the domain of hockey's ruling snipers, the coveted Hart Trophy has rarely been awarded to defensemen or goalies. So when rearguards, such as Bobby Orr and Eddie Shore, have been honoured as league MVP, it's special. No different was Pratt's influence on the game. He was the only Original Six defenseman to win the celebrated Hart (1944), after scoring 57 points to set a blue-liner record that stood for 21 years.

3.10   A. Harry Howell

Howell was the kind of player that improved with age. He toiled on the Rangers' blueline for 15 seasons before compiling his best offensive record (40 points) and landing an All-Star team appointment and the Norris as top defenseman in 1967. Of the 1,050 scheduled games during that stretch, Howell played in 1,030. Over the years, his blueline partners included greats such as Allan Stanley, Bill Gadsby and Doug Harvey. But no one impressed Howell like Bobby Orr, the 1966–67 rookie Howell paid tribute to in his Norris acceptance speech: "I am glad I won the Norris this year, because in 10 years it will be called the Bobby Orr Trophy."

3.11 **D. Red Kelly (as a Red Wing)**

The last time a D-man nailed gentlemanly play honours was in 1954, when Kelly won his third Lady Byng with Detroit. Defense is a tough position to play while avoiding penalties, and Kelly was among the few NHL rearguards who combined playmaking excellence with clean hockey, finishing sixth with 49 points and only 18 minutes in penalties.

The NHL's Last Lady Byng-Winning Season by a Defenseman • Red Kelly, 1953–54

Player	Team	GP	G	A	PTS	PIM
G. Howe	Detroit	70	33	48	81	109
M. Richard	Montreal	70	37	30	67	112
T. Lindsay	Detroit	70	26	36	62	110
B. Geoffrion	Montreal	54	29	25	54	87
B. Olmstead	Montreal	70	15	37	52	85
R. Kelly	Detroit	62	16	33	49	18

3.12 **B. Doug Harvey**

Harvey won his seventh (and final of eight seasons) top defenseman award in 1961–62, the year he was player/coach of the Rangers. New York finished fourth in the final standings and Harvey notched 30 points.

HOCKEY CROSSWORD

(Solutions are on page 131)

Across

1. Montreal's No. 16 in drawing
3. _____ Baun
5. _____ shot
8. "_____ and grind"
10. _____ Worsley
11. _____ Boivin
12. _____ Ross
13. Metro _____
14. _____ a standing ovation
17. _____ Litzenberger
20. Advice
22. _____ in the right position
23. "_____ the puck"
25. Opponent. The _____ team
28. 2nd chance on goal
31. Manager Tommy _____
34. Empty or _____ net
35. Soft touch
36. Reggie _____
38. "_____ Glorieux"
40. Hawk hometown
42. Pinpoint _____
45. Montreal's Ken _____
47. Team proprietor
48. He shoots, _____ scores
49. _____ Reibel
51. _____ McDonald
54. _____ office
55. Goalie Al _____
57. The six-team _____
58. "_____ sir!"
59. Camille, the _____, Henry

Down

1. _____ Laycoe
2. Consecutive game player
3. Boston's Bobby _____
4. _____ Guidolin
5. Chicago's Pat _____
6. _____ Rollins
7. Cool, ready to play
8. Toe _____
9. Detroit, the _____ City
15. Player's money man
16. Goalie _____
18. _____ Clapper
19. Hold on to puck
21. _____ Goyette
22. _____ Broda
24. Detroit's Jack _____
26. "Odds or _____ "
27. Slam
29. Play _____.500 hockey
30. "_____-time the puck"
32. "_____ play"
33. Nimble
36. Hall of _____
37. The League
39. Illegal tactic with stick
41. The _____ Jet
43. Al _____
44. Toronto's Sid _____
46. _____ DeJordy
48. _____ Cain
50. Detroit's Sid _____
52. "Changing on the _____ "
53. "Illegal _____ of the stick"
54. Devotee
56. Jean Béliveau, _____ Gros Bill

SCORING RECORDS
AND REWARDS

MOST OF THE OFFENSIVE and defensive records set during the 50- 60- 70-game schedules of the six-team era have long since been erased by the achievements that followed league expansion in 1967. But the marks established long ago by Original Six players such as Rocket Richard, Bill Durnan and Gordie Howe remain measures of excellence today. These men were the first to become 50-goal scorers, shutout streak wonders and consecutive scoring title champions in a talent-rich league compressed into the six-team format.

(Answers are on page 46)

4.1   **If Wayne Gretzky broke Gordie Howe's goal-scoring record (801 goals) and Howe broke Maurice Richard's (544 goals), whose total-goal record did Richard break in 1952? (And what goal total was broken?)**
A. Syl Apps
B. Nels Stewart
C. Bill Cook
D. Howie Morenz

4.2   **Who was the first player to break the 50-goal barrier?**
A. Maurice Richard
B. Bernie Geoffrion
C. Bobby Hull
D. Gordie Howe

4.3 **How many scoring titles did Gordie Howe win during the six-team era between 1942 and 1967?**
A. Two titles
B. Four titles
C. Six titles
D. Eight titles

4.4 **How many minutes of shutout hockey did goalie Bill Durnan play in the longest shutout sequence of the six-team era?**
A. 120 to 180 minutes—under three games
B. 180 to 240 minutes—under four games
C. 240 to 300 minutes—under five games
D. More than 300 minutes

4.5 **When Terry Sawchuk equalled George Hainsworth's NHL record of 94 shutouts in Detroit's 3–0 win over the Canadiens on November 10, 1963, what other hockey milestone was set during that same game?**
A. Gordie Howe broke Maurice Richard's 544-goal record
B. The Canadiens played their 2,500th game, an NHL first
C. Jean Béliveau scored his 1,000th career point
D. Future hero of the Canada-Soviet Summit Series, Paul Henderson, scored his first NHL goal in his first league game with the Red Wings

4.6 **Who was the ironman of the six-team era?**
A. Johnny Wilson
B. Alex Delvecchio
C. Harry Howell
D. Andy Hebenton

4.7 **Who holds the record for the fastest hat trick in NHL history?**
A. Max Bentley
B. Bobby Hull
C. Bill Mosienko
D. Jean Béliveau

4.8 **Who set up all three goals to help establish the NHL's fastest hat trick record?**
A. Clint Smith
B. Gus Bodnar
C. Doug Bentley
D. Bill Gadsby

4.9 **What is the fastest goal by a rookie in his first NHL game?**
A. Less than 30 seconds
B. Between the 1:00- and 2:00-minute mark
C. Between the 2:00- and 5:00-minute mark
D. More than five minutes

4.10 **Who is the only Original Six skater to win hockey's triple crown—the Art Ross, Hart and Lady Byng Trophies in one season?**
A. Bobby Hull
B. Jean Béliveau
C. Stan Mikita
D. Andy Bathgate

4.11 **Terry Sawchuk holds the NHL record for most regular-season shutouts during the six-team era. Who holds the record for most playoff shutouts?**
A. Jacques Plante
B. Turk Broda
C. Glenn Hall
D. Terry Sawchuk

4.12 **How many times did Gordie Howe score 50 goals in one season during the six-team era?**
A. Never
B. Once
C. Three times
D. Five times

4.13 **Which Canadiens star was booed by Montreal fans after he won the NHL scoring title in 1955?**
A. Dickie Moore

B. Bernie Geoffrion
C. Jean Béliveau
D. Maurice Richard

4.14 **Which NHLer during the six-team era received the most penalty minutes in one season?**
A. Ted Lindsay
B. John Ferguson
C. Howie Young
D. Reg Fleming

4.15 **Which NHL record does Maurice Richard still hold outright?**
A. Most goals, one playoff game
B. Most points, one playoff period
C. Most overtime goals, one playoff year
D. Most overtime goals in playoffs, career

4.16 **Who was the only NHLer during the six-team era to tie Maurice Richard's record for most points in one game?**
A. Howie Meeker
B. Max Bentley
C. Dave Keon
D. Bert Olmstead

4.17 **Who was the first NHLer to record multiple 50-goal seasons?**
A. Bobby Hull
B. Bernie Geoffrion
C. Maurice Richard
D. Phil Esposito

4.18 **What is the fastest time one player has scored two goals in playoff action?**
A. Five seconds
B. 15 seconds
C. 25 seconds
D. 35 seconds

SCORING RECORDS
AND REWARDS

4.1 **B. Nels Stewart**
Known as "Old Poison," Stewart proved the dead-accuracy of his shots each game. He was the first NHLer to score 300 goals. After a celebrated 15-year career playing on the Maroons' popular S Line and tours with Boston and the New York Americans, Stewart retired in 1940 with an all-time league-record 324 goals. It stood for 12 years, until Richard fired his 325th beyond the Hawks' Al Rollins on home ice November 8, 1952. The Forum shook with thunderous applause, followed by the staccato of popping flash bulbs. Play was halted and Richard picked up the landmark puck. In recognition, Stewart sent a telegram: "Congratulations on breaking the record. Hope it will hold for many seasons."

4.2 **C. Bobby Hull**
Richard first scored 50 goals in 1945; then Geoffrion in 1961, and Hull in 1962. But it wasn't until the 5:34 mark of the third period on March 12, 1966, that Hull pulled the trigger on the Rangers' Cesare Maniago to smash the 50-goal barrier. Seven minutes of pandemonium filled Chicago Stadium as 22,000 fans celebrated. The Golden Jet had out-rocketed Rocket Richard with the NHL's first 51st goal. It came off a Lou Angotti assist in Hull's 56th game. Hull would score another the next night and peak with 54 goals by season's end.

4.3 **C. Six titles**
Howe won the Art Ross Trophy as the league's scoring leader six times, including four-in-a-row between 1950

and 1954, another in 1956–57, and his last, in his 17th NHL season (1962–63), when he was 35. Even in his 40s, Gordie was still challenging for the Art Ross, finishing third against such superstars as Bobby Hull and Phil Esposito in the late 1960s. The only NHLer with more scoring championships than Howe's six-pack is Wayne Gretzky, who owns 10 Art Ross titles.

4.4   **D. More than 300 minutes**
Durnan's shutout streak began at 16:15 of the first period on February 24, 1949, against Chicago, and continued through four complete games (Feb. 26: Detroit 1–0; Mar. 2: Toronto 2–0; Mar. 5: Boston 4–0; and Mar. 6: Boston 1–0) before ending on another Hawk goal at 5:36 of period two on March 9, 1949: 309 minutes and 21 seconds of shutout performance by Durnan with stellar defense work from the Canadiens' rearguards Kenny Reardon, Doug Harvey and Butch Bouchard.

4.5   **A. Gordie Howe broke Maurice Richard's 544-goal record**
Hainsworth's shutout record endured for more than a quarter-century of hockey. Richard's offensive mark was fated to belong to Howe. When and where were the only questions. Both NHL records, owned by Montreal players, were equalled and passed on November 10, 1963, by two Red Wings. Ironically, it occurred against Hainsworth and Richard's former team, the Canadiens. Sawchuk blanked Montreal 3–0 for his 94th SO and Howe scored goal number 545 against Charlie Hodge, breaking Richard's mark.

4.6   **D. Andy Hebenton**
Hebenton played in 630 consecutive games over nine complete 70-game seasons for New York and Boston from 1955–56 through 1963–64. The next best Original Six ironman record is 580 games, held by Detroit's Johnny Wilson, who played every game from February 10, 1952, to March 20, 1960.

Bill Mosienko, the man who scored hockey's fastest hat trick.

4.7   **C. Bill Mosienko**

The Blackhawks played ugly for much of the 1951–52 season (17–44–9), until their last game on March 23, 1952, when Mosienko pumped in three rapid-fire goals in 21 seconds on New York goalie Lorne Anderson. The miracle hat trick came at 6:09, 6:20 and 6:30 of the third period, with both teams at full strength and Chicago down 6–2. The game didn't mean much, but the inspired play of Mosienko gave a bit of lustre to the dismal season while producing a 7–6 win. It also spelled the end for Anderson, who never backstopped in the NHL again. Mosienko's hat trick broke Carl Liscombe's record, set in 1938 when the Detroit rookie scored three goals in 1:52. The second-fastest hat trick is 44 seconds, scored by Jean Béliveau on November 5, 1955.

4.8   **B. Gus Bodnar**

Mosienko's 21-second hat trick happened after Chicago's centre, Bodnar, won three successive face-offs and passed for three assists to establish the historic trio of goals.

4.9   **A. Less than 30 seconds**

Gus Bodnar, the same man who assisted on the NHL's fastest hat trick, also holds another "fastest" league record—the quickest goal by a rookie. Bodnar, in his first NHL game, scored 15 seconds after the first puck was dropped on October 30, 1943. His victim was the Rangers' rookie netminder, Ken McAuley, also appearing in his first NHL game.

4.10   **C. Stan Mikita**

Chicago's No. 21 for 22 seasons, Mikita is the only player to win the Art Ross as leading scorer, the Hart as league MVP and the Lady Byng as top nice guy—all in the same season (1966–67). His 70-game totals pushed him 17 points ahead of runner-up Hull in the scoring derby, and his 12 penalty minutes total was among the league's lowest. Remarkably, he repeated his triple crown the following season, in 1967–68.

Mikita's First Triple-Trophy Season • 1966–67

Player	Games	Goals	Assists	Points	PIM
Stan Mikita	70	35	62	97	12
Bobby Hull	66	52	28	80	52
Norm Ullman	68	26	44	70	26
Ken Wharram	70	31	34	65	21
Gordie Howe	69	25	40	65	53

4.11   **D. Terry Sawchuk**

"The Shutout King" blanked the opposition a record 11 times during 13 playoff seasons. His best post-season was 1952, when Detroit swept Toronto and Montreal in eight straight games. Sawchuk netted four zeros for a stingy 0.62 goals per game average, and limited the Canadiens to a meagre two goals in the Cup finals. The next best NHL playoff record belongs to Plante, with 10 shutouts in 11 seasons.

4.12   **A. Never**

Despite the numerous records established during his illustrious 26-year career, Gordie never cracked the elusive 50-goal mark, set by Maurice Richard. However, according to linemate Sid Abel, in 1952–53, the 49-goal year, Howe did pop his 50th on a tip-in from a Red Kelly shot in Boston on March 19th, 1953. Howe didn't argue the call, as he expected to get number 50 in one of the season's two final games, in Chicago or Montreal. But the Hawks held Howe scoreless and the big showdown against Richard's team evolved into a grudge match, as the Canadiens draped Howe with defenders to prevent him from tying the Rocket. The tactic worked, thwarting Howe's chance for 50. Still, Mr. Hockey had won his third straight Art Ross Trophy—by a 24-point margin—and the Hart Trophy as league MVP.

4.13 B. Bernie Geoffrion

Why would the hometown crowd boo Geoffrion, especially after he had won the coveted NHL scoring title? The answer lay in the emotional suspension of Maurice Richard for a stick-swinging incident, which cost the Canadiens star the last three games of the 1954–55 season (and the playoffs). Until then, the scoring race was a point-for-point, game-by-game struggle among three elite Canadiens: Richard, Geoffrion and Jean Béliveau, with both Big Jean and the Boomer only points behind the Rocket. After the nightmarish events that unfolded following Richard's suspension, with Canadiens fans rioting, looting stores and overturning cars in downtown Montreal, Geoffrion racked up three crucial points in the final games, enough to unseat the almighty Richard (and make the hockey gods in Montreal very unhappy). The suspension and riots were a black eye for the game, and Geoffrion's title turned into a crown of thorns; his coronation into a crucifixion. As he stepped onto Forum ice at the start of the 1955 playoffs, thousands booed, taking out their frustration over Richard's suspension on the Art Ross Trophy winner. It would be years before Habs fans forgave Geoffrion's "act of treason." Worse, it turned out to be Richard's only chance at a scoring title. As for Béliveau, he knew better, and wisely finished one point back of the Canadiens' greatest hockey player ever.

The 1954–55 NHL Final Scoring Standings

Player	Team	GP	G	A	Pts	PIM
B. Geoffrion	Montreal	70	38	37	75	57
M. Richard	Montreal	67	38	36	74	125
J. Béliveau	Montreal	70	37	36	73	58
E. Reibel	Detroit	70	25	41	66	15
G. Howe	Detroit	64	29	33	62	68

4.14 **C. Howie Young**

Up until 1962–63, the NHL penalty stat sheets were ruled by bad guy Lou Fontinato. His bruising 202 minutes in 1955–56 made Fontinato the reigning king of the box, and the only NHLer to amass plus 200 minutes in one year. But that changed on February 17, 1963. Young, battling his way through every game against every team, turned a high-sticking incident into a full-blown tantrum and was assessed a major, a minor, a misconduct and a game misconduct totalling 27 minutes—enough to jack his season penalty totals to 208 minutes. League president Clarence Campbell suspended Young for three games; his own team, Detroit, announced an indefinite suspension. Young's reinstatement a few days later enabled him to compile more box time, ending his season with an unprecedented 273 minutes.

4.15 **D. Most overtime goals in playoffs, career**

Even after more than three decades of retirement, Richard's name still dots the NHL record books. The Rocket is tied for a few records (including multiple-choices A, B and C), but the most significant mark that remains unequalled today is his six playoff overtime goals: one scored in 1946, three in 1951, one in 1957 and one in 1958.

4.16 **D. Bert Olmstead**

Although many post-expansion shooters have equalled the eight-point record Richard established in 1944 (broken by Darryl Sittler's remarkable 10-point game in 1976), only Olmstead did it during the six-team era, notching four goals and four assists on January 9, 1954, in a 12–1 drubbing over Chicago. It happened almost exactly 10 years after Richard's scoring outburst on December 28, 1944.

4.17 **A. Bobby Hull**

Although Richard and Geoffrion each compiled 50-goal seasons before Hull, no sniper had ever scaled the NHL

Bobby Hull slaps another blistering 100 m.p.h. shot.

scoring race to twice reach that lofty plateau. Only years earlier, the 50-goal season was an unassailable mark, idealized through the enduring images of a streaking Rocket Richard and others, including Gordie Howe, who had come so close. Now, Hull was poised to match hockey's grandest offensive achievement. This kid, with a muscular physique that reflected his farming roots in Port Anne, Ontario, turned slapshots into missiles and rushes into spectacular blitzes while amassing four consecutive 50-goal seasons (he added a fifth in 1971–72). Hull became the league's single greatest attraction and ambassador of the game.

The NHL's First 50-Goal Scorers

Player	Date	Goaltender	Game No.	Age
M. Richard	March 18, 1945	H. Bennett	50	23.7
B. Geoffrion	March 16, 1961	C. Maniago	62	30.1
B. Hull	March 25, 1962	G. Worsley	70	23.2
B. Hull	March 2, 1966	H. Bassen	52	27.2
B. Hull	March 18, 1967	B. Gamble	63	28.2
B. Hull	March 5, 1969	E. Giacomin	64	30.2
P. Esposito	Feb. 20, 1971	D. DeJordy	58	29.0

4.18 **A. Five seconds**

On April 11, 1965, Detroit's Norm Ullman scored the two fastest goals in Stanley Cup history, beating Glenn Hall at 17:35 and 17:40 of the second period in a 4–2 win over Chicago. Ullman's pair came with the Wings behind 2–1. Detroit won the game, but eventually lost the series in seven.

THE AMAZING DOZEN

Only 12 NHLers (see clues below) won the scoring race during hockey's Golden Age. Reading across, down or diagonally, find the Art Ross Trophy winners by connecting lines between the letters in their names, for example, B-E-N-T-L-E-Y. Do not use any letter more than once and start with the letters in heavy type. (Hint: Both Bentley brothers won scoring championships.) *(Solutions are on page 132)*

First Name Clues:

Max _____	Herb _____	Doug _____
Elmer _____	Roy _____	Ted _____
Gordie _____	Bernie _____	Jean _____
Dickie _____	Bobby _____	Stan _____

	E	L	T	C	E	
Y	U	H	O	N	B	L
L	L	N	H	E	R	A
T	A	C	O	W	H	C
I	A	H	G	E	N	N
K	U	Y	E	A	I	O
A	I	M	E	O	C	I
E	I	L	M	L	F	R
V	E	N	O	O	T	F
B	I	D	Y	R	E	N
	L	S	A	E	B	

WHO AM I?

WHAT MADE THE ORIGINAL SIX era so special was its simplicity... and familiarity. Six teams played each other 14 times, seven at home and seven away. Rivalries quickly developed into long-standing feuds between players and teams. Fans knew every player and his position in the league. Kids easily collected the entire set of NHL trading cards. And almost everyone could tell you who was the first NHL player to score 100 goals against all opposing teams.

In this chapter we revive the spirit of old-time hockey and test your memory without multiple-choice clues. Simple. By the way, Gordie Howe was the first NHLer to score 100 goals against all opposition. The last club to surrender? The Canadiens and goalie Gump Worsley on February 7, 1965.

(Answers are on page 59)

5.1 I was the first player in NHL history (followed by Wayne Gretzky and Eric Lindros) to finish tied in the NHL scoring race, but lose the Art Ross Trophy as top point leader because I had fewer goal totals than my opponent. It happened in 1961–62. *Who am I?*

5.2 I played defense and forward from 1953 to 1975 in 1,390 games, both with Boston and, later, with Chicago, where I had my best years as linemate to Stan Mikita and Kenny Wharram. *Who am I?*

5.3 When I joined the Bruins in my rookie year, 1942–43, at age 16, I was the youngest player in NHL history. *Who am I?*

5.4 I am the only Hall-of-Famer to receive "lifetime banishment" from the NHL. *Who am I?*

5.5 In 1959–60 I played a hell of a season, my best, battling the great Bobby Hull for the NHL scoring race. We tied in total goals, but he won the Art Ross Trophy, beating me by one assist. *Who am I?*

5.6 As brothers, we formed a complete offensive line— a feat not repeated until Quebec put Peter, Marion and Anton Stastny together as linemates in 1981. It happened in the 1940s. *Who are we?*

5.7 I was the last goalie to play every minute of every game in a regular season. It happened in 1963–64. *Who am I?*

5.8 So I got mad and slugged a referee! Unfortunately, they hit me back with the largest fine ever handed out to an individual in NHL history to date. It happened in 1961. *Who am I?*

5.9 Despite finishing in the fourth (and last) playoff position in the 1948–49 regular-season standings, we won the Stanley Cup. *Who are we?*

5.10 I led the NHL with five shutouts in 1946–47, but my team failed to make the playoffs. *Who am I?*

5.11 I potted the first sudden-death goal ever scored in a seventh game overtime of a Stanley Cup final series. It happened in 1950. *Who am I?*

5.12 Good news and bad news! I played only one game in my NHL career. The good news? Hey, my only appearance was with a Stanley Cup-winning team in the Cup finals. *Who am I? (Hint: Detroit, 1950.)*

5.13 When Bernie Geoffrion scored his 50th in 1961, equalling Maurice Richard's record, I was the goalie. When Bobby Hull broke the 50-goal mark in 1966, guess who was in nets? Me! *Who am I?*

5.14 I am the youngest goalie in NHL history. My career began in 1943 with Detroit and I played for each of the Original Six clubs except Montreal. *Who am I?*

5.15 I was the first player from a losing side to win the Conn Smythe Trophy as playoff MVP. *Who am I?*

5.16 Years after winning rookie of the year honours, Chicago offered my team $1 million for my services. That was big money in the early 1960s, but the deal was turned down. After a few Stanley Cups, I played in Detroit and Montreal, where I won more Cups in the 1970s. *Who am I?*

5.17 I got my first taste of playoff action tending goal for Boston in 1957, but my biggest post-season thrill came with Toronto in 1962. I replaced an injured Johnny Bower and beat Chicago in the last two games of the finals to lead the Leafs to their first Cup since 1951. *Who am I?*

Answers

W H O   A M   I ?

5.1   Despite scoring 84 points to tie Bobby Hull in the NHL scoring race in 1961–62, **Andy Bathgate** lost the Art Ross Trophy because Hull scored more goals—52 to 28.

5.2   **Doug Mohns** played 11 seasons with Boston, using his great checking skills to move between defense and left wing. His aggressive, hard-working style netted him a 20-goal season before he was traded in 1964–65 to Chicago, where he produced four more 20-goal years playing with Mikita and Wharram. Mohns had the endurance of a horse, concluding his solid 22-year career with Minnesota, Atlanta and Washington.

5.3   As World War II raged, NHL ranks suffered. As many as half of all the league regulars were recruited for the war, forcing team managers to find replacements—whatever their age or experience. Enter **Armand "Bep" Guidolin**, who joined the threadbare Bruins a month shy of his 17th birthday in November 1942, making him the youngest NHLer ever. When the boys returned from the war, many took back their former playing positions, leaving others without a skating job. But that didn't happen to Bep, who earned his stripes in a pro career that spanned nine years with Boston, Detroit and Chicago. Later, he coached the Bruins and Kansas City Scouts.

5.4   **Babe Pratt**, hockey's leading defenseman of the 1930s and early 1940s, was banished from the league for gambling on Maple Leaf games. After considering his status and his plea for reconsideration, the league's board of governors looked the other way and Pratt was back skating on Maple Leaf ice just nine games after his "lifetime banishment."

Bronco Horvath, the unknown who almost beat Bobby Hull in the NHL scoring race.

5.5   **Joseph "Bronco" Horvath** came out of nowhere, exploded onto the NHL scoring sheets and, almost overnight, disappeared. After five years in the minors and two unimpressive NHL seasons, Boston coach Milt Schmidt combined Horvath with Johnny Bucyk and Vic Stasiuk on the Bruins' Uke Line. In 1957–58, they racked up 174 points, Horvath scoring 30 goals and 36 assists. But Horvath's best season came in 1959–60, when he battled Hull for the scoring title. The race was a nail-biter, eventually coming down to the season's final match between Chicago and Boston, with Horvath ahead of Hull by one point (a goal). In the first period, Horvath left the game and was taken to hospital after a puck hit his face. Hull, with room to breath, turned it on and scored a goal and an assist, gaining a one-point advantage. Horvath heroically returned for the last period of the season, but no matter how many plays his teammates set up or how loud the Bruins fans roared, he couldn't put one behind Glenn Hall. Tied with 39 goals each, Hull won the Art Ross by one assist. Bronco, it was later revealed, set an NHL record for scoring in 22 successive regular-season games. Final season point total: Hull 81 points, Horvath 80 points. Horvath scored an impressive 326 career points in 434 NHL games, but never lived up to the superstar potential he displayed during the season he lost the scoring race by one point to Bobby Hull.

5.6   On New Year's Day, 1943, Chicago coach Paul Thompson introduced the all-Bentley line, playing brothers **Max, Doug and Reg Bentley** together as a unit against the Rangers. It was the first time three brothers were linemates in an NHL game. The Hawks defeated New York 6–5, but the novel experiment failed to click and the trio was soon broken up.

5.7   Boston's **Eddie Johnston** was the last goalie to play every minute of an NHL season when he backstopped the Bruins for all 4,200 minutes, or 70 complete games, in 1963–64.

5.8 Furious after a disallowed goal by his Canadiens, an over-time Hawk power play and the ensuing Chicago game-winner in triple overtime in the 1961 playoffs, Montreal coach **Toe Blake** jumped the bench and bareknuckled referee Dalton McArthur. Blake got nailed for $2,000, the largest NHL fine ever. In addition, league president Clarence Campbell stipulated that Blake must pay the fine personally, without team assistance.

5.9 The **Toronto Maple Leafs** surprised everyone in 1948–49: first, by finishing in fourth place after two consecutive Stanley Cups (1947 and 1948), then, by winning the Cup a third straight time after such an uneven regular season (22–25–13). Coach Hap Day's boys mobilized timely offense with sturdy defense to produce three NHL firsts: the first fourth-place finisher to win the Cup, the only Original Six team under .500 to do so and the first triple Stanley Cup winner.

5.10 **Chuck Rayner** took little solace in beating puckstopping peers Bill Durnan and Turk Broda with his league-leading five shutouts in 1946–47, particularly since his Rangers failed to mount enough offense to make the playoffs. It's no wonder he tried potting a few himself. In the dying seconds on January 25, 1947, with Broda out of the net, Rayner rushed 30 feet for a loose puck and fired it up the ice, almost scoring a goal. His rink-long dashes drew standing ovations, but did little to inspire his teammates. New York ended their season in fifth place with a 22–32–6 record.

5.11 Third-line winger **Pete Babando** didn't play many seasons or pot a lot of playoff goals (only three) in his short career, but the one he scored on April 22, 1950, made up for all the shots that missed; it will be remembered forever as the first Stanley Cup-winning goal scored in overtime. Babando waited for the right moment to be the unlikely hero. The shot came off a George Gee pass and

sailed beyond stunned New York goalie Chuck Rayner at
28:31 of double overtime, creating bedlam at Detroit's
Olympia. For the Rangers, who finished 21 points behind
the Wings in the regular season, their Cinderella playoff
story was over.

5.12 **Doug McKay** is the only player whose lone NHL game was
with a Cup winner in the Stanley Cup finals. It happened
during the 1950 Stanley Cup when McKay was a member
of the Detroit Red Wings.

5.13 Never winning the Stanley Cup or any individual trophy
while solidly backstopping some ordinary teams, **Cesare
Maniago's** 15 seasons did produce a couple of highlights.
Unfortunately, they weren't in recognition of his fine
play, but of someone else's: first, being victimized by
Geoffrion's 50th, then, Hull's 51st to break the all-time
record. Maniago also gave up Esposito's third 50th goal
in 1974.

5.14 **Harry "Apple Cheeks" Lumley** was signed by Detroit
when he was only 16, and started his first NHL game at age
17 on December 22, 1943, losing to Chicago 7–1. Lumley
played two more games that season, including one the following night *against* his Detroit teammates when New
York "borrowed" him after their goalie, Ken McAuley,
went down. Lumley lost again, 5–3. It would be the only
occasion the future All-Star netminder played for the
Rangers in an outstanding 16-year career that took him to
every one of the Original Six teams except Montreal.

5.15 When **Roger Crozier** was named playoff MVP in 1966, the
Detroit netminder established himself as both the first
goalie and first player from a losing side to win the Conn
Smythe. Backstopped by Crozier, the fourth-place Wings
surprised everyone in the playoffs. After losing 11 of 14
regular-season games to the Hawks, Detroit took the
semi-finals 4–2 in games, then, in Montreal, won back-to-

back games at the Forum against the heavily-favoured Canadiens. Crozier played brilliantly to keep the Detroit hopes alive, but the bubble burst and the next four games belonged to Montreal. Despite losing the Cup, Crozier won the Conn Smythe, posting a stellar 2.17 goals-against average.

5.16 **Frank Mahovlich** established his goal-scoring credentials in 1957–58 as the league's rookie of the year. After he scored 48 goals in 1960–61, the Blackhawks offered Toronto $1 million for Mahovlich. But the Leafs nixed the deal. Detroit later picked up the Big M in 1968, when most figured his best years were behind him. League expansion and the change of address rejuvenated Mahovlich, who turned in some of his most productive scoring years for Detroit, then capped his career by collecting a couple of Stanley Cups with Montreal in the 1970s.

5.17 When Toronto picked up Boston goalie **Don Simmons** in 1961, the Leafs knew exactly what they wanted: a seasoned number one playoff goalie who could play solid backup to Bower in any given game situation. It was a prophetic move by Toronto general manager Punch Imlach. During the 1962 Cup finals, Bower pulled a leg muscle while stretching for a wicked shot by Bobby Hull. Simmons filled the breach and demonstrated his coolness under pressure, winning the Stanley Cup in back-to-back victories, 8–4 and 2–1, against the defending Cup champion Blackhawks.

THE GORDIE HOWE NUMBERS GAME

Gordie Howe holds more Original Six records than any other NHLer. Many of his personal bests, including most goals in one season, were set prior to 1967 expansion. Match the numbers listed below with Howe's league records (LR) and personal records (PR).

(Solutions are on page 132)

4   8   9   11   12   18   21   49   91

109   156   649   825   1,398   1,501

1._____ Most Regular Seasons (LR)

2._____ Most Points/Playoffs (LR)

3._____ Most Goals/Season (PR)

4._____ Most +30-Goal Seasons (LR)

5._____ Most Assists/Career (LR)

6._____ Most Points/Career (LR)

7._____ Fastest Goal/Seconds (LR)

8._____ Most Penalties/Season (PR)

9._____ Most +40-Goal Seasons (LR)

10._____ Most Games/Career (LR)

11._____ Most Assists/Playoffs (LR)

12._____ Most Points/Finals/1 Year (LR)

13._____ Most Goals/Career (LR)

14._____ Most +20-Goal Seasons (LR)

15._____ Most Goals/Semi-finals/1 Year (LR)

Chapter SIX

MASKS OF COURAGE

AMONG THE MANY developments that shaped hockey during the six-team era, perhaps none is more important than Jacques Plante's goalie mask. If the crude, thin fibreglass shell had been half as durable as the much-criticized Plante, it would have been made of the strongest substance known to man. Courage, maybe. The mask was introduced at a time when shooters were perfecting the 100 m.p.h. slapshot. Without protection, barefaced goalies were in grave peril. Here are some other puckstopping achievements worthy of strapping on the pads. *(Answers are on page 71)*

6.1 **Who is the goalie shown on the facing page?**
A. Detroit's Terry Sawchuk
B. Boston's Eddie Johnston
C. Detroit's Roger Crozier
D. Chicago's Glenn Hall

6.2 **What was Chicago goalie Al Rollins' win-loss-tie record in 1953–54, his Hart Trophy-winning season, as league MVP?**
A. 12–47–7
B. 22–37–7
C. 32–27–7
D. 42–17–7

6.3 **Before the tandem goalie system, how did goaltenders who received a major penalty serve their penalties?**

A. The penalized goalie served a one-game suspension

B. A penalty shot was awarded to the opposing team

C. The penalized goalie was fined

D. The penalized club substituted a skater in the penalty box

6.4 **Who was the first goalie to win 40 games in a season?**

A. Terry Sawchuk

B. Jacques Plante

C. Turk Broda

D. Glenn Hall

6.5 **What is the highest number of total career points any one goalie scored during the six-team era?**

A. Under 10 points

B. Between 10 and 15 points

C. Between 15 and 20 points

D. More than 20 points

6.6 **How many consecutive complete games, regular-season and playoff, did Chicago goalie Glenn Hall play during his famous ironman streak?**

A. Between 200 and 300 games

B. Between 300 and 400 games

C. Between 400 and 500 games

D. Between 500 and 600 games

6.7 **Which goalie recorded the most shutouts in one season? How many SOs did he amass?**

A. Glenn Hall

B. Terry Sawchuk

C. Harry Lumley

D. Jacques Plante

6.8 **How many games did Jacques Plante lose in two playoff rounds in 1960, the first post-season he wore his mask?**

A. None

B. Two games
C. Four games
D. Six games

6.9 **What was the age of the oldest goalie ever to appear in an NHL game?**
A. 40 years
B. 42 years
C. 44 years
D. Over 45 years

6.10 **What is the highest goals-against average for a goalie (with 30 or more games in one season)?**
A. Between 4.00 and 5.00 goals-against
B. Between 5.00 and 6.00 goals-against
C. Between 6.00 and 7.00 goals-against
D. Between 7.00 and 8.00 goals-against

6.11 **Who did Detroit have in their lineup to replace Stanley Cup-winning goalie Terry Sawchuk in 1955?**
A. Glenn Hall
B. Al Rollins
C. Harry Lumley
D. Johnny Bower

6.12 **How long did Charlie Hodge play backup goaltender with the Canadiens organization before he became Montreal's number one man between the pipes?**
A. One playoff game
B. One season
C. Three seasons
D. Nine seasons

6.13 **How many of Terry Sawchuk's record 103 shutouts occurred during the six-team era?**
A. 70 to 79 shutouts
B. 80 to 89 shutouts
C. 90 to 99 shutouts
D. 100 or more shutouts

6.14 **What is the longest shutout streak ever recorded by one goalie in the Stanley Cup finals? (With or without overtime, each game lasts 60 minutes; two games, 120 minutes; three games, 180 minutes, etc.)**
A. Between 90 and 120 minutes (about two games)
B. Between 120 and 150 minutes (more than two games)
C. Between 150 and 180 minutes (almost three games)
D. More than 180 minutes (at least three games)

6.15 **Which six-team era goalie is the only netminder to appear in at least 60 playoff games and compile a goals-against average of under 2.00 (lifetime)?**
A. Frank Brimsek
B. Turk Broda
C. Glenn Hall
D. Jacques Plante

6.16 **Which Original Six goalie recorded the most penalty minutes?**
A. Harry Lumley
B. Gump Worsley
C. Terry Sawchuk
D. Jacques Plante

6.17 **Who was the last goalie to win the Hart Trophy as league MVP?**
A. Ed Giacomin
B. Johnny Bower
C. Harry Lumley
D. Jacques Plante

6.18 **Who was the last Original Six goalie to retire?**
A. Tony Esposito
B. Rogatien Vachon
C. Al Smith
D. Gerry Cheevers

MASKS OF COURAGE

6.1 **C. Detroit's Roger Crozier**
Widespread acceptance of the mask didn't occur overnight. Despite the risks, barefaced goalies such as Crozier were still ducking and dodging rubber in 1965. It was a Calder Trophy-winning year for the Wings rookie netminder, who led Detroit to a first-place finish with six shutouts and a 2.42 goals-against average.

6.2 **A. 12–47–7**
Chicago's only reprieve from total embarrassment during their disastrous 1953–54 season (12–51–7) was the phenomenal work of Rollins, who, despite playing for a team that surrendered 242 goals (60 more than any other club), recorded a 3.23 goals-against average and four shutouts in 12 Hawk victories. Chicago finished last to achieve the dubious honour of most season losses (51) during the six-team era, but Rollins won the Hart as MVP.

6.3 **B. A penalty shot was awarded to the opposing team**
Prior to 1949, goalies who received major infractions would face a penalty shot. The NHL rule was revised after the 1949 playoffs, when referee King Clancy declined to invoke the major-penalty-shot rule in sudden-death overtime, after a scuffle between Ken Reardon and goalie Harry Lumley. Clancy, a former NHL star, did banish Reardon on a hooking penalty and the Red Wings scored on the power play.

6.4 **A. Terry Sawchuk**
Sawchuk was the first goaltender to win 40 games, a feat he accomplished in 1950–51—his rookie year! In the 70-game schedule, his 44 wins included 11 shutouts and a

miserly 1.99 goals-against average, second only to Bernie Parent's NHL all-time record of 47 wins in 1973–74's 78-game schedule. Sawchuk won the 1951 Calder Trophy as rookie of the year for his efforts. The following season, Sawchuk won 44 games again and his first Vezina Trophy as best puckstopper. Amazingly, Sawchuk never averaged above 2.00 goals-against in his first five full years.

Sawchuk's Early Years • 1950–55

Year	Team	GP	GA	SO	GAA
1950–51	Detroit Red Wings	70	139	11	1.99
1951–52	Detroit Red Wings	70	133	12	1.90
1952–53	Detroit Red Wings	63	120	9	1.90
1953–54	Detroit Red Wings	67	129	12	1.94
1954–55	Detroit Red Wings	68	132	12	1.96

6.5   A. Under 10 points

Under old hockey systems, job definitions were simple and clear-cut: forwards passed and scored goals, defensemen defended and goalies knew their place was inside the crease making saves. Except for the occasional talented rushing defenseman, few questioned the game plan, and goalies almost never passed up-ice to score assists. (Although some goalies did "rack up" points, they never scored more than two in a season.) In 17 years, Terry Sawchuk amassed six assists; Glenn Hall, six; and Jacques Plante, four.

6.6   D. Between 500 and 600 games

Hall holds hockey's record of records, one that will never be broken. He began his streak as a Detroit rookie, on October 6, 1955, and ended as a Blackhawk with back pain on November 7, 1962; 502 regular-season games and 49 playoff matches without missing a night's work. Incredible! Seven years of continuous play and 551 consecutive complete games.

The NHL Record of Records • Hall's Streak Years

Year	Team	Games	W	L	T	GA	SO	GAA
1955–56	Wings	70	30	24	16	148	12	2.11
	Playoffs	10	5	5	0	28	0	2.80
1956–57	Wings	70	38	20	12	157	4	2.24
	Playoffs	5	1	4	0	15	0	3.00
1957–58	Hawks	70	24	39	7	202	7	2.89
	Playoffs	—	—	—	—	—	—	—
1958–59	Hawks	70	28	29	13	208	1	2.97
	Playoffs	6	2	4	0	21	0	3.50
1959–60	Hawks	70	28	29	13	180	6	2.57
	Playoffs	4	0	4	0	18	0	4.50
1960–61	Hawks	70	29	24	17	180	6	2.57
	Playoffs	12	8	4	0	27	2	2.25
1961–62	Hawks	70	31	26	13	186	9	2.66
	Playoffs	12	6	6	0	31	2	2.58
Nov. 1962	Hawks	12	5	3	4	29	1	2.42
Totals		**551**	**235**	**221**	**95**	**1430**	**50**	**2.60**

6.7 **C. Harry Lumley**

Lumley won a Stanley Cup with the 1949–50 Red Wings, but his best years came in Toronto, where he iced 1.85 (1953–54) and 1.94 (1954–55) averages. He won the Vezina Trophy in 1954, his career year, and stymied the opposition a record-breaking 13 times in the 70-game schedule. No goalie in the six-team era bettered Lumley's SO mark, not even Sawchuk, who posted three 12-shutout seasons (1951–52, 1953–54 and 1954–55).

6.8 **A. None**

Plante, who introduced his self-designed face protector in 1959, was the first goalie in hockey history to wear a mask in the Stanley Cup. He did it with the right team (a squadron of Cup-seasoned superstars) in the most convincing way, first in the semi-finals against Chicago and, later, versus Toronto, winning the Cup in eight straight victories. Finally, the critics were silenced. Plante's scintillating performance—he allowed only five goals in the Cup finals' four games—led to worldwide acceptance of the mask as standard puckstopping equipment.

6.9   D. Over 45 years

Johnny Bower, at 45, is regarded as the oldest netminder to strap on the pads for an NHL game. Yet he could not equal Moe Roberts, a Chicago trainer and former goalie who, at age 46, was called in to replace an injured Harry Lumley on November 24, 1951. It was Roberts's first NHL game in 17 years and he served his professional calling with honour, shutting down the Wings in the third period to preserve a 6–2 lead for the Hawks win.

6.10   C. Between 6.00 and 7.00 goals-against

"A bad year" is too kind a description for the season New York had in 1943–44. They set an unenviable record by posting 39 losses in the 50-game schedule, subjecting Ken "Tubby" McAuley to a defense so porous he set the NHL's all-time highest single-season goals-against average: 6.20 goals per game. McAuley played another dismal season (4.93 GAA) for the Rangers, who only found new hope (a.k.a. Chuck Rayner) when the boys came marching home from Europe in 1945.

6.11   A. Glenn Hall

Hall played backup in Detroit for two seasons (1952–53 and 1953–54) before snagging full-time work between the Wings' pipes, after Detroit boss Jack Adams dealt Sawchuk to the Bruins in 1954. Hall posted a red-hot 2.11 GAA and copped the Calder Trophy as top rookie. Yet, despite a second strong season in 1956–57, the Red Wings never regained their Stanley Cup form with Hall.

6.12   D. Nine seasons

With regulars Plante, Bower, Hall, Sawchuk and Worsley filling NHL puckstopping positions during most of the six-team era, job prospects for other netminders were, at best, slim. Some goalies waited, played a few NHL games, bussed around the minors and then, maybe, bought a lucky break somehow. Such was the sorry journey of Jacques Plante's backup, Hodge, who, over nine seasons with the Montreal franchise, played just 59 NHL games. Some years Hodge never joined the big team at all, putting in time in the AHL, EPHL, QHL, QSHL AND WHL. But that changed when Plante was dealt to New York in 1963. Hodge's patience paid off. His skills never sharper (and his new defense awesome), he worked 62 games, recorded eight shutouts for a 2.26 goals-against average and won the Vezina Trophy as top goalie.

Charlie Hodge's Nine-Year Reality Check

Year	Team	League	GP	GA	SO	GAA
1952–53	Mtl. Royals	QSHL	1	4	0	4.00
1953–54	Buffalo	AHL	3	10	0	3.33
1954–55	Mtl. Royals	QHL	35	113	2	3.23
1954–55	Canadiens	NHL	13	31	1	2.27
1954–55	Providence	AHL	5	18	1	3.60
1955–56	Seattle	WHL	70	239	6	3.41
1956–57	Rochester	AHL	41	132	2	3.22
1956–57	Shawinigan	QHL	14	39	2	2.79
1957–58	Canadiens	NHL	12	31	1	2.58
1957–58	Mtl. Royals	QHL	48	153	4	3.19
1958–59	Canadiens	NHL	2	6	0	3.00
1958–59	Rochester	AHL	4	12	0	3.00
1958–59	Mtl. Royals	QHL	24	67	1	2.79
1959–60	Royals/Hull	EPHL	59	170	7	2.88
1959–60	Canadiens	NHL	1	3	0	3.00
1960–61	Mtl. Royals	EPHL	22	74	0	3.38
1960–61	Canadiens	NHL	30	76	4	2.53
1961–62	Quebec	AHL	65	185	5	2.85
1962–63	Quebec	AHL	67	190	4	2.84
1963–64	Quebec	AHL	10	32	1	3.20
1963–64	Canadiens*	NHL	62	140	8	2.26

* Won Vezina Trophy as NHL's top goalie.

6.13   **D. 100 or more shutouts**

Prior to NHL expansion, Sawchuk played in a record 914 games with Detroit, Boston and Toronto, recording 100 shutouts from 1949 through 1967. Only three of his league-leading 103 shutouts were notched during the post-expansion years, including his last SO on February 1, 1970.

6.14   **D. More than 180 minutes (at least three games)**

Toronto's Frank McCool was unbeatable for 188:35 minutes in the 1944–45 Toronto–Detroit finals. To set the NHL Stanley Cup record, McCool shut down the Red Wings' attack in each of the first three games, relinquishing his first goal at 8:35 of the first period in game four. (Detroit rebounded to beat McCool in the next three matches, setting up game seven, which Toronto won 2–1 to claim the Cup. It was McCool's last final series.)

6.15   **B. Turk Broda**

He was the quintessential "money" goalie: a good puckstopper during the regular season (2.54 GAA), but great under pressure in the playoffs. He won five Stanley Cups (between 1936 through 1952) and logged the NHL's lowest goals-against average (1.98 goals per game in postseason). Broda is the only puckstopper in NHL history with +60 playoff games below 2.00.

The Original Six Clutch Goalies' Lifetime Playoff Averages

Player	GP	GA	SO	GAA
T. Broda	102	211	13	1.98
J. Plante	112	241	15	2.17
H. Lumley	76	199	7	2.50
T. Sawchuk	106	267	12	2.54
J. Bower	74	184	5	2.54
F. Brimsek	68	186	2	2.56
G. Hall	115	321	6	2.79

"The Shutout King,"
Terry Sawchuk.

6.16 **C. Terry Sawchuk**
He was intense, though temperamental; competitive, but moody; and talented, however unorthodox. And that's what made Sawchuk the goaltending force behind so many NHL awards and records, including penalty minutes leader among netminders with 229 minutes (39 PIM in 1957–58), rink-lengths ahead of Worsley (101), Lumley (89) and Plante (84).

6.17 **D. Jacques Plante**
At least nine goalies (Tony Esposito, Ken Dryden and Grant Fuhr among them) have earned enough votes to claim runner-up as league MVP, but the last puckstopper to win the Hart was Jacques Plante in 1962. The Canadiens' goalie played all 70 games, topping all net-

minders with a sparkling 2.37 goals-against average and leading Montreal to a 42–14–14 record, 13 points ahead of second-place Toronto. Plante also won his sixth Vezina Trophy in seven seasons.

6.18 **B. Rogatien Vachon**
Al Smith manned the nets from 1965 to 1981, in an NHL career that began with the Maple Leafs and ended in Colorado. Cheevers played from 1961 to 1980 with Toronto, Cleveland (WHA) and Boston. Esposito quit in 1984, but never tended goal during the six-team era. Vachon, who began in 1966–67 with Montreal, survived 17 seasons with Los Angeles, Detroit and Boston before burying the pads in 1981–82.

STANLEY CUP HEROES

The honour of playing in the Stanley Cup goes to those lucky few who realize their dreams by competing at a level of skill and intensity beyond even *their* expectations. Self-possessed and unyielding, players of different backgrounds and all qualifications go to the Cup finals with one ambition: To be number one.

The 37 winning coaches, captains, goalies and Cup-winning goal scorers listed below appear in the puzzle—horizontally, vertically, diagonally or backwards. Some are easily found, like Dick I-R-V-I-N, others require a more careful search. After you have circled all 37 names, read the remaining letters in descending order to spell the veteran goaltending team that won the last Stanley Cup of the Original Six era. *(Solutions are on page 133)*

APPS	GEOFFRION	McDONALD
ARMSTRONG	HALL	McNEIL
BABANDO	HODGE	MOORE
BARILKO	HOWE	PILOUS
BATHGATE	IRVIN	PLANTE
BÉLIVEAU	IVAN	PRATT
BONIN	KENNEDY	PRIMEAU
BOUCHARD	LACH	RICHARD
BRODA	LESWICK	SHACK
DAVIDSON	LITZENBERGER	SIMMONS
DAY	LUMLEY	SKINNER
DUFF	McCOOL	WORSLEY
GARDNER		

```
O                                              P
K                                              R
L                                              I
I                                              M
R                                              E
A                                              A
B  R O D A                                     U
R E N N I K S N O S D I V A D B Y Y            Y
E G D O H C B O U C H A R D L E E P
N R F O C A L O O C C M Y I L L R N
D E F W A H A L L B S D E M S A I D
R B U E L S R S A T E N U R T V E L
A N D R A H C I R N C L O T R W R A
G E O F F R I O N M C W I I H E O N
A Z B O N I N E T N A L P V W U O O
P T Y A D G K C I W S E L O E K M D
P I L O U S I M M O N S H I V A N C
S L E T A G H T A B A B A N D O U M
```

NICKNAMES AND
OTHER TALES

F EW EPOCHS IN HOCKEY have produced better nicknames
for players and forward units than the six-team era. Oh
sure, The Philadelphia Flyers' "Legion Of Doom" ranks
high on the list, but there was a certain richness and spirit to the
Motor City's feared trio, "The Production Line," and such
monikers as "Leapin' Lou" and "Old Lamplighter." Even the
era, remembered as The Original Six and The Golden Age, con-
veys a sense of epic privilege. In this chapter we revive great
nicknames of the past and a few events long forgotten.

(Answers are on page 87)

7.1 **Who was "Leapin' Lou"?**
A. Lou Angotti
B. Louie Fontinato
C. Leo Boivin
D. Lou Nanne

7.2 **Who is shaking hands with Toronto's Ted Kennedy
on the facing page?**
A. The future Queen of England
B. The 1952 world figure skating champion
C. Lady Byng, wife of Canada's Governor General
D. The new owner of the Detroit Red Wings

7.3 **Which Canadiens star said to his bride: "Someday, I'll score more goals than your father did."?**
A. Jean Béliveau
B. Bernie Geoffrion
C. Ralph Backstrom
D. Henri Richard

7.4 **Who played on Chicago's "Scooter Line"?**
A. Ab McDonald–Stan Mikita–Kenny Wharram
B. Reggie Fleming–Tod Sloan–Eric Nesterenko
C. Elmer Vasko–Pierre Pilote–Dollard St. Laurent
D. Bobby Hull–Bill Hay–Murray Balfour

7.5 **Who was the first NHLer to make the cover of _Sports Illustrated_?**
A. Bobby Hull
B. Gordie Howe
C. Maurice Richard
D. Jean Béliveau

7.6 **Who was "Old Lamplighter"?**
A. Roy Conacher
B. Ted Kennedy
C. Max Bentley
D. Toe Blake

7.7 **What was hockey's so-called "Battle of the Bulge"?**
A. The 1949 Toronto–Detroit Stanley Cup finals
B. A weight-loss order issued to overweight players
C. The on-ice rivalry between Ted Lindsay
   and Maurice Richard
D. An NHL-sponsored campaign to buy Allied War Bonds

7.8 **Who was nicknamed "Clark Kent" on the Maple Leafs?**
A. Kent Douglas
B. Andy Bathgate
C. Tim Horton
D. Eddie Shack

7.9 **Which Boston general manager engineered "The Trade," sending Pit Martin, Gilles Marotte and Jack Norris to Chicago in exchange for Phil Esposito, Ken Hodge and Fred Stanfield?**
A. Lynn Patrick
B. Hap Emms
C. Milt Schmidt
D. Harry Sinden

7.10 **Who was the first on-ice official to use hand signals?**
A. Cooper Smeaton
B. Conn Smythe
C. Bill Chadwick
D. Chaucer Elliott

7.11 **Who was considered hockey's fastest skater?**
A. Henri Richard
B. Bobby Hull
C. Ted Lindsay
D. Bernie Geoffrion

7.12 **Who are Mr. and Mrs. Lou Reese?**
A. The married couple that founded the Hockey Hall of Fame
B. The parents of Jeff Reese, the only NHL goalie with three assists in one game
C. The only married couple who have their names on the Stanley Cup
D. The married couple who got hit by separate pucks during an NHL game

7.13 **Who earned the nickname "Terrible Ted"?**
A. Ted Lindsay
B. Ted Harris
C. Ted Green
D. Ted Kennedy

7.14 **Who was "Handy Andy"?**
A. Andy Hebenton
B. Ed Van Impe
C. Andy Bathgate
D. Andre Pronovost

7.15 **Who was the first coach to remove his goalie during a delayed penalty?**
A. Montreal's Dick Irvin
B. Toronto's Hap Day
C. Boston's Milt Schmidt
D. Detroit's Tommy Ivan

7.16 **Who was the "Dipsy Doodle Dandy from Delisle" (Saskatchewan)?**
A. Frank McCool
B. Marty Pavelich
C. Al Arbour
D. Max Bentley

7.17 **Why was Toronto's "Flying Forts Line" given that name?**
A. The entire line came from Fort William, Ontario
B. All three linemates played over the age of 40
C. Each linemate played junior hockey in Fort Francis, Ontario
D. The linemates lived as rookies in a Toronto hotel, known as Fort Knox

Answers

NICKNAMES AND OTHER TALES

7.1   **B. Louie Fontinato**
Not a Hall-of-Famer by any standard, Fontinato was the kind of character player every team wanted for strength and ruggedness across the blueline, and needed when the gloves came off. When he joined the league in 1954, the New York press immediately dubbed him "Leapin' Lou" for his running and jumping skating style. They soon discovered his prime asset: he compiled just 104 points while amassing 1,247 penalty minutes in 535 NHL games. Perhaps his most memorable heavyweight bout came in 1959 when he challenged Gordie Howe, who broke Lou's nose and smashed his face with several lefts and rights. By the time the Ranger brawler delivered three of his own best shots, without inflicting any damage, he knew the fight was lost. Howe's last powerful uppercut knocked Leapin' Lou senseless. Fontinato played rugged and fearless for nine years with New York and Montreal before his career ended tragically in 1963, when he broke his neck crashing headlong into the boards on a check to the Rangers' Vic Hadfield. Leapin' Lou recovered, as he always did, but never played hockey again.

7.2   **A. The future Queen of England**
Two years before her coronation as monarch of the British Empire, Princess Elizabeth and her husband, Philip, the Duke of Edinburgh, watched a 1951 exhibition game at Maple Leaf Gardens. The Leafs' captain, Kennedy, paid his respects rinkside before the match.

Bernie "Boom-Boom" Geoffrion on the night he scored number 270 to equal the great Howie Morenz in goals.

7.3 **B. Bernie Geoffrion**

Ten years after Geoffrion married Howie Morenz's daughter, Marlene, Geoffrion's prediction came true. On December 7, 1960, the Boomer blasted home his 270th and 271st NHL goals, which equalled and passed the career goal totals of his father-in-law, the legendary Morenz.

7.4 **A. Ab McDonald–Stan Mikita–Kenny Wharram**

Favoured with an abundance of talented players, Chicago coach Rudy Pilous juggled the Hawk lineup until he formed an early version of the "Scooter Line" of Hull–Hay–Balfour (soon called the "Million-Dollar Line"), with speedsters Hay and Balfour coming over from Montreal. But Chicago's real "Scooter Line" was veteran Wharram, sophomore centre Mikita and ex-Hab McDonald, whom Pilous put together in 1960–61. The Scooter Line motored its way into hockey's lexicon during the 1961 Stanley Cup championship and continued for years as one of the league's most productive scoring units. In 1963–64, the line accounted for almost half of Chicago's goals.

7.5 **D. Jean Béliveau**

Despite the phenomenal popularity and widespread press coverage of the rivalries between the game's two best players, Howe and Richard, Béliveau got the big ink and landed the *Sports Illustrated* cover on January 23, 1956, two years after the magazine was first published, in 1954.

7.6 **D. Toe Blake**

Blake acquired his nickname, "Old Lamplighter," from the red goal lights (or lamps) he ignited so routinely in his early playing days with the Maroons and the Canadiens. Even before the Punch Line with Maurice Richard and Elmer Lach, Blake was a Stanley Cup winner, a league scoring champ and an MVP winner of the Hart Trophy. As senior linemate and Montreal captain, he directed the Canadiens to two Cups (1944 and 1946). Later, he continued his winning ways behind the bench, coaching

Montreal to an unprecedented eight championships, a record five-in-a-row in his first five seasons (1956 to 1960). Beyond the accolades and silverware, Blake was a teacher, whose captaincy was beyond reproach; his on-ice presence and resolve was a measure of both his skills and leadership. As a coach, Toe was tough and demanding. Former Canadiens have often said: "Blake didn't know what the word 'lose' meant, because it wasn't in his vocabulary." In all, Blake won 11 Stanley Cups. He made the best players better and, ultimately, showed the next generation of coaches, such as Scotty Bowman and Mike Keenan, how to win.

7.7   B. A weight-loss order issued to overweight players

When the members of his reigning champion Maple Leafs ballooned to non-athletic proportions in 1949, Toronto boss Conn Smythe ordered the portly players on a weight-reduction program that some press scribes called the "Battle of the Bulge." Vic Lynn, Harry Watson and Howie Meeker were all targeted, but goalie Turk Broda, Smythe's main porker, was ordered to trim 10 pounds in one week. To prove his seriousness, the Leaf manager called up goalie Gil Mayer from the minors and bought Al Rollins from the AHL Cleveland Barons. It worked. The players shed the fat; Broda even weighed in under his limit of 190 pounds. Back in shape, the Leafs finished third and Broda recorded a career-high nine shutouts. Not bad, considering that many thought Smythe's weight-loss program was just another one of his publicity stunts.

7.8   C. Tim Horton

With his horn-rimmed glasses and tremendous athletic strength, Horton was the Superman of the Leafs during the 1960s. Some teammates thought him fearless. He was Toronto's backbone, an inspirational leader with a clean, hard-hitting defensive style, who could turn a game around with one of his patented end-to-end rushes.

Horton was a solid competitor and intimidated opponents with skill and strength, not dirty tactics. He brought the game honour each night he played. He was a natural.

7.9   C. Milt Schmidt

A member of Boston's storied Kraut Line with Woody Dumart and Bob Bauer during the Bruins' Stanley Cup years of 1939 and 1941, Schmidt orchestrated another Cup-winning event on May 15, 1967. Robbing Chicago of Esposito, Hodge and Stanfield (coupled with Bobby Orr's arrival) turned the basement-dwelling Bruins into Stanley Cup champions in three seasons, while the Hawks dive-bombed from first place to fourth before crashing into the NHL cellar.

7.10   C. Bill Chadwick

In the mid-1940s, Hall of Fame referee Bill Chadwick developed his own hand gestures to indicate, both to players and fans, what penalty had been called. By 1946–47, all NHL referees and linesmen were using official hand signals adopted by the league.

7.11   B. Bobby Hull

It's been said that Hull combined the skills of hockey's greatest superstars—the speed of Howie Morenz, the scoring touch of Maurice Richard and the strength, endurance and puck control of Gordie Howe. In his 23-year career, Hull consistently dominated both the NHL and WHA scoring sheets, but perhaps the most dazzling aspect of his game—next to his blistering slapshot—was his skating, clocked full-tilt at 29.7 m.p.h., or 28.3 m.p.h. with a puck.

7.12   D. The married couple who got hit by separate pucks during an NHL game

March 28, 1943, was a busy night in the Red Wings' infirmary, not for injured players, but for the fans in attendance—and one married couple in particular. First, Mrs.

Reese took four stitches after being struck in the face by a puck. Then, moments after she returned to her seat, another stray puck cut her husband for two stitches. The Wings won 4–2 over Toronto.

7.13 **A. Ted Lindsay**

So just how "Terrible" was Detroit's Ted Lindsay? By the time his 17-year NHL career ended in 1964–65, Lindsay had served nearly 2,000 penalty minutes, the most box time of any Original Six player. He had battled through many epic fights and earned numerous fines for his stick-work. It is said he stopped counting the number of stitches in his face after he reached 400. But his aggressive, fearless approach to the game doesn't begin to describe the superior quality of Lindsay's hockey skills, nor the immeasurable difference he made as Detroit's physical and emotional leader. His contribution to the Wings' Production Line brought Detroit four Stanley Cups between 1950 and 1955, and netted Lindsay the Art Ross Trophy as 1949–50's scoring leader. He was named to the first All-Star team as best left winger eight times. Lindsay was one of hockey's most ferocious competitors, as his numbers indicate: 379 goals, 851 points and 1,808 penalty minutes in 1,068 games.

7.14 **C. Andy Bathgate**

Bathgate proved his handiness many times over with the Rangers, leading the team in scoring for nine successive years while missing only five games. But scoring sprees and ironman marks alone can't describe the hockey skills possessed by Bathgate. His all-round abilities combined finesse as a stickhandler and skater with a devastating slap-shot, playmaking gamesmanship with off-ice leadership, and longevity achieved with bad knees. Bathgate played 17 years, challenged Gordie Howe and won the Hart as league MVP (1959), equalled Bobby Hull in the NHL scoring race (1961–62) and collected a Stanley Cup with Toronto (1964). His contribution to the game, undiminished by bigger-name players, has stood the test of time.

Andy Bathgate holds the stick he used to net goal number 33 in 1958–59, equalling a Ranger record set by Bill Cook.

7.15 C. Boston's Milt Schmidt

The Bruins didn't have to be losing late in the game for Schmidt to pull his goalie—he was known to add an extra attacker in the offensive zone with five seconds remaining, no matter the period or the score. So the next logical offensive move? Pull your goalie for an extra skater during a delayed penalty. The opposition couldn't score because any play on their part would be immediately whistled "dead." On October 20, 1960, Schmidt introduced what would become standard hockey strategy by pulling goalie Don Simmons and adding forward Bronco Horvath after referee John Ashley signalled a delayed penalty against Detroit. Boston didn't score, but they held the extra offensive punch for 10 seconds before the whistle.

7.16 D. Max Bentley

Broadcaster Foster Hewitt first described Bentley as a "dipsy doodler" because of his dazzling on-ice moves. It wasn't long before some fertile mind lengthened the alliteration and dubbed the well-attired Saskatchewan native the "Dipsy Doodle Dandy from Delisle."

7.17 A. The entire line came from Fort William, Ontario

The "Flying Forts Line" was formed in 1943–44 when rookie Gus Bodnar joined two other Fort William natives, Gaye Stewart and Bud Poile (both Maple Leaf sophomores), to became part of Toronto's rebuilding scheme. In 1947, manager Conn Smythe traded the entire line (plus others) in the "trade of the century" to get Chicago scoring champ Max Bentley, and Cy Thomas.

L I S T E N   U P !

After an unknowing soul asked Jacques Plante if wearing a mask proved he was scared, the facemask inventor remarked: "If you jumped out of a plane without a parachute, would that make you brave?"

Match the following memorable quotes and their authors.

(Solutions are on page 133)

Ted Lindsay (1950s)
Turk Broda (1940s)
Phil Esposito (1967)
Olympia PA Announcer (1950s)

Bep Guidolin (1942)
Conn Smythe (1957)
Maurice Richard (1963)
Glenn Hall (1961)

1. _____ "Octopi shall not occupy the ice. Please refrain from throwing same."

2. _____ "The Leafs pay me for my work in the practices, and I throw in 60 games for nothing."

3. _____ "Geez, sir, do you know I'm only 16?"

4. _____ "It's always nice to score against the team that traded you."

5. _____ "Those guys have laughed at us long enough."

6. _____ "He's a great player. How about that, scoring both his 544th and 545th against my old team."

7. _____ "The stick is a great equalizer for me."

8. _____ "If he had a team made up of Rocket Richard and four more like him, he still couldn't win." (Describing Howie Meeker.)

T E A M W O R K

I N 1956–57, THE NHL ENACTED a rule that allowed penalized players to return to the ice when a goal was scored by an opposing team. That rule, still used today, was originally created to prevent Original Six powerhouses like the Montreal Canadiens from blowing out the opposition over the stretch of a two-minute penalty. In one such 1955 game, Montreal scored three power play goals in 44 seconds. In this chapter we celebrate teamwork: four lines of offense, three pairs of defense, goaltending, speciality teams and coaching.

(Answers are on page 100)

8.1 **What Original Six team scored the most goals in one season?**
A. The Toronto Maple Leafs, 1946–47
B. The Detroit Red Wings, 1950–51
C. The Montreal Canadiens, 1961–62
D. The Chicago Blackhawks, 1966–67

8.2 **What team traded Terry Sawchuk in 1957?**
A. The New York Rangers
B. The Toronto Maple Leafs
C. The Boston Bruins
D. The Detroit Red Wings

8.3 **When the 1984–85 Edmonton Oilers broke the record for the longest undefeated streak (from start of season), what Original Six team's record did they smash?**

A. The Montreal Canadiens, 1943–44
B. The Toronto Maple Leafs, 1946–47
C. The Detroit Red Wings, 1950–51
D. The Toronto Maple Leafs, 1962–63

8.4 **What are the fewest number of points to separate the top four teams in the NHL's final standings? (And in what year did it happen?)**

A. Five points
B. 10 points
C. 15 points
D. 20 points

8.5 **What is the most consecutive goals scored by one team in an NHL game?**

A. Seven straight goals
B. 10 straight goals
C. 12 straight goals
D. 15 straight goals

8.6 **Which Original Six team gave up the most goals-against in a season?**

A. The Boston Bruins
B. The New York Rangers
C. The Chicago Blackhawks
D. The Montreal Canadiens

8.7 **Which Original Six club finished in first place most often?**

A. The Montreal Canadiens
B. The Toronto Maple Leafs
C. The Chicago Blackhawks
D. The Detroit Red Wings

8.8 What NHL trade between two teams for opposing net-minders resulted in (within one season) one club receiving the Vezina Trophy winner (for best goalie) and the other club, the Hart Trophy winner (for league MVP)?

A. Montreal's Jacques Plante for New York's Gump Worsley

B. Detroit's Glenn Hall for Chicago's Terry Sawchuk

C. Chicago's Harry Lumley for Toronto's Al Rollins

D. Toronto's Gerry Cheevers for Boston's Don Simmons

8.9 What minor league club did Bobby Hull play for before joining Chicago?

A. None. Hull jumped directly from Junior A to the Blackhawks

B. The Hawks' AHL franchise in Buffalo

C. The Hawks' WHL affiliate in Los Angeles

D. The Hawks' CPHL affiliate in St. Louis

8.10 Which NHL club first painted their gloves to match their uniform colours?

A. The Toronto Maple Leafs

B. The Detroit Red Wings

C. The New York Rangers

D. The Montreal Canadiens

8.11 Name the only Original Six team to finish in first place without placing a scorer among the top 10 scoring leaders.

A. The Boston Bruins

B. The Detroit Red Wings

C. The New York Rangers

D. The Toronto Maple Leafs

8.12 Which non-NHL team challenged the league for the Stanley Cup in 1953?

A. Colorado College

B. The Michigan Wolverines

C. The 1952 Soviet National team

D. The Cleveland Barons

8.13 Just before Red Kelly was traded to Toronto in 1960, he was involved in another deal that fizzled on Detroit manager Jack Adams. Which team did Kelly almost play for instead of Toronto?

A. The New York Rangers

B. The Montreal Canadiens

C. The Boston Bruins

D. The Chicago Blackhawks

8.14 Which teams featured the Pony Line, the Production Line, the Punch Line and the Uke Line? (Match each forward unit with the four teams below.)

A. The Detroit Red Wings

B. The Boston Bruins

C. The Chicago Blackhawks

D. The Montreal Canadiens

8.15 How many club(s) recorded 100-point regular seasons during the six-team era? And which club did it first?

A. One team. Montreal

B. Two teams. Detroit first, followed by Montreal

C. Two teams. Montreal first, followed by Toronto

D. Three teams. Toronto first, followed by Detroit and Montreal

8.16 Which club produced the most scoring champions during the six-team era?

A. The Montreal Canadiens

B. The Detroit Red Wings

C. The Toronto Maple Leafs

D. The Chicago Blackhawks

T E A M W O R K

8.1 D. The Chicago Blackhawks, 1966–67
With Hawk snipers Stan Mikita, Bobby Hull, Kenny Wharram and Phil Esposito amassing 139 goals and snatching four of the top seven NHL scoring positions, Chicago recorded an NHL-high 264 goals to celebrate their first regular-season championship and the Blackhawks' 40th anniversary as an NHL franchise.

8.2 C. The Boston Bruins
On July 24, 1957, Boston received Detroit sophomore Johnny Bucyk in exchange for Sawchuk, who had backstopped the Bruins for two solid seasons (goals-against average: 1955–56: 2.66; 1956–57: 2.38). Sawchuk (plus Vic Stasiuk and Marcel Bonin) had come to the Bruins in the 1955 trade that sent Warren Godfrey, Réal Chevrefils and Ed Sandford to Detroit.

8.3 A. The Montreal Canadiens, 1943–44
It was the most successful Canadiens season ever, beginning with an undefeated streak of 14 games (11w–3T) led by Maurice Richard, Elmer Lach and Toe Blake, bluelined by captain Emile Bouchard and backstopped by Vezina Trophy-winner, Bill Durnan. The Canadiens were virtually unstoppable, losing an NHL-record five games in a league ravaged by World War II recruiting, which claimed players from every position and team. Montreal, the least affected club, capitalized and finished first with 38 wins and 83 points, producing the greatest point spread (25 points) between first- and second-place teams during the six-team era. Montreal's undefeated streak (from start of season) stood for 41 years.

8.4   **A. Five points**
1962–63 was the tightest regular-season race in NHL history. When the dust settled, only five points separated the league's top four teams. It went down to the wire as Chicago kept pace with the Leafs, but failed to take advantage of Toronto's poor showing late in the season. The Leafs managed only one point in their final three games. Chicago couldn't do any better, picking up just three points in its last five matches.

The NHL's Tightest Race • 1962–63 Standings

Team	GP	W	L	T	GF	GA	PTS
Toronto	70	35	23	12	221	180	82
Chicago	70	32	21	17	194	178	81
Montreal	70	28	19	23	225	183	79
Detroit	70	32	25	13	200	194	77
New York	70	22	36	12	211	233	56
Boston	70	14	39	17	198	281	45

8.5   **D. 15 straight goals**
It's been called the "most lopsided game in NHL history." No team scored more consecutive goals in one game than Detroit, which on January 23, 1944, whipped the hapless Rangers 15–0. Victimized in the onslaught was New York goalie Ken McAuley, who faced a sea of red sweaters all night and a barrage of 58 shots on goal. In fact, the Rangers didn't win another game all season. Detroit's 15-goal record stands today; as does McAuley's NHL record 6.20 goals-against average (30 or more games).

8.6   **B. The New York Rangers**
The 1943–44 Blueshirts were surely the worst team in the club's long and illustrious history. Their 6–39–5 record affirmed how the calibre of hockey had declined in the NHL during the war years. Gone from the Rangers' lineup were

Lynn Patrick, Phil Watson, Clint Smith, Alf Pike and Dud Garrett. Things were so desperate that manager Lester Patrick wanted to suspend operations, and coach Frank Boucher laced up the skates after six years of retirement. Nonetheless, the Rangers, who went winless in their first 15 starts, attracted crowds in excess of 15,000 at Madison Square Garden, a clear sign that professional hockey provided a welcome boost for a nation suffering from the strain of four years at war. At season's end, the Rangers totalled 310 goals-against, more than any other NHL team until the California Golden Seals surrendered 320 goals in 1970–71. Of course, the Seals set their mark in a 78-game schedule; the Rangers, in just 50 games.

8.7   A. The Montreal Canadiens
While the Red Wings hold the NHL's all-time record for consecutive first-place finishes with seven (1948–49 through 1954–55), Montreal registered 12 regular-season championships between 1942 and 1967; ahead of Detroit (10), Toronto (2) and Chicago (1).

8.8   C. Chicago's Harry Lumley for Toronto's Al Rollins
In the 1952 swap, Toronto picked up Lumley, whose record 13 shutouts in 1953–54 earned him the Vezina; Chicago pulled in the 1954 MVP-winner, Rollins.

8.9   A. None. Hull jumped directly from Junior A to the Blackhawks
As crucial as Stan Mikita, Pierre Pilote and Glenn Hall were to rebuilding the Blackhawks franchise into a Stanley Cup contender and eventual winner, the most important player to step over Chicago's boards in the late 1950s was Hull. His sparkling career in Junior A with the St. Catherines TeePees (33–28–61 in 52 games in 1955–56) won him a tryout at Chicago's 1957 training camp. Hull's strength, speed, stickhandling and shot were so exceptional, he turned pro at 18 without spending a day in the minors.

8.10 **C. The New York Rangers**
In 1957–58 the Rangers were the first NHL team to decorate their standard natural-coloured gloves, painting them red, white and blue to match their uniforms. The last hold-out among Original Six clubs were the Red Wings, who waited until 1967.

8.11 **B. The Detroit Red Wings**
The only Original Six team to finish first overall without a Top Ten scorer was the 1942–43 Red Wings. Detroit compiled the league's second-worst goal total, but registered the best goals-against by a 35-goal margin. Detroit's leading scorer was Syd Howe with 55 points, almost 20 points off the lead and 12th in rank. Defense proved the difference. Goalie Johnny Mowers captured the Vezina Trophy as top goalie in the regular season and recorded an exemplary 1.94 goals-against in the post-season, including two shutouts at Boston Garden to ice the Stanley Cup. Not bad for a team without big gunners.

8.12 **D. The Cleveland Barons**
According to Lord Stanley's original guidelines, written when he donated the Cup in 1892, the AHL's Cleveland Barons had every right to challenge the NHL and the Stanley Cup winners. But being the sole proprietors of Lord Stanley's "bowl" and possessing the best hockey players in the world, the NHL said "no thanks," and refused the invitation to play against what the league considered to be a lower calibre team. In 1953, the Barons boasted such talents as Johnny Bower, Fred Shero and coach Bun Cook.

8.13 **A. The New York Rangers**
Before the 1960 Toronto deal, Detroit manager Jack Adams traded Kelly (and Bill McNeill) to New York in exchange for Bill Gadsby and Eddie Shack. But Kelly refused to report to the Rangers. The deal was nixed and the Simcoe, Ontario, native soon found himself homeward bound to Toronto and the Maple Leafs.

Maurice Richard, Elmer Lach and Toe Blake: Montreal's fabled "**Punch Line**."

8.14 **A. The Detroit Red Wings**
The Production Line, with Ted Lindsay, Sid Abel and Gordie Howe.
B. The Boston Bruins
The Uke Line, with Johnny Bucyk, Vic Stasiuk and Bronco Horvath.
C. The Chicago Blackhawks
The Pony Line, with Doug Bentley, Max Bentley and Bill Mosienko.
D. The Montreal Canadiens
The Punch Line, with Toe Blake, Elmer Lach and Maurice Richard.

8.15 **B. Two teams. Detroit first, followed by Montreal**
One year after 70-game schedules were adopted
(1949–50), teams began recording the first 100-point seasons. But not with any consistency. In fact, only two
Original Six clubs had +100-point seasons. Detroit
accomplished the feat twice, collecting 101 points in
1950–51 (44w–13l–13t) and 100 points in 1951–52
(44w–14l–12t), before the Canadiens' lone 100-point
year in 1955–56 (45w–15l–10t). Although Montreal
placed second to Detroit in points, the Canadiens ranked
higher in wins, an NHL-record 45 games in 1955–56, compared to the Wings' best effort of 44 victories in 1950–51
and 1951–52.

8.16 **D. The Chicago Blackhawks**
Chicago demonstrated beyond a doubt that scoring leaders
do not guarantee Stanley Cups. Despite leading the NHL
with 10 scoring champs between 1942 and 1967, the
Hawks won just one Stanley Cup.

Original Six Teams with the Most Scoring Champs

Player Titles	Team	Scoring Champions
10	Chicago	Doug Bentley (1), Max Bentley (2), Roy Conacher (1), Bobby Hull (3), Stan Mikita (3)
7	Detroit	Ted Lindsay (1), Gordie Howe (6)
7	Montreal	Elmer Lach (2), Bernie Geoffrion (2), Jean Béliveau (1), Dickie Moore (2)
1	Boston	Herb Cain (1)

THE CUP WINNERS

The object is to determine the Stanley Cup winners in each year, given that one team won 10 championships (hint: including five-in-a-row), another club won nine, a third team won five, a fourth team won one and two teams saw no silver during the six-team era.

(Solutions are on page 134)

Year	Finalists	Cup Winner
1942–43	Boston vs. Detroit	_____
1943–44	Montreal vs. Chicago	_____
1944–45	Toronto vs. Detroit	_____
1945–46	Montreal vs. Boston	_____
1946–47	Montreal vs. Toronto	_____
1947–48	Detroit vs. Toronto	_____
1948–49	Toronto vs. Detroit	_____
1949–50	New York vs. Detroit	_____
1950–51	Toronto vs. Montreal	_____
1951–52	Montreal vs. Detroit	_____
1952–53	Boston vs. Montreal	_____
1953–54	Montreal vs. Detroit	_____
1954–55	Detroit vs. Montreal	_____
1955–56	Montreal vs. Detroit	_____
1956–57	Boston vs. Montreal	_____
1957–58	Montreal vs. Boston	_____
1958–59	Montreal vs. Toronto	_____
1959–60	Toronto vs. Montreal	_____
1960–61	Detroit vs. Chicago	_____
1961–62	Chicago vs. Toronto	_____
1962–63	Toronto vs. Detroit	_____
1963–64	Detroit vs. Toronto	_____
1964–65	Montreal vs. Chicago	_____
1965–66	Detroit vs. Montreal	_____
1966–67	Toronto vs. Montreal	_____

Chapter NINE

TRUE OR FALSE?

WITH ONLY 120 PLAYER positions available each season, rookies had a hard time making it during the six-team era, and veterans faced an even more difficult challenge in trying to stave off the next hockey generation. Everyone played hurt, and frequently even injured. Failure to routinely compete in top form every night could mean banishment and a pro career spent in the minors. Perhaps that's why most of the NHL's 20-year men come from the Original Six. They weren't about to give up the struggle that had brought them so far.

In this section, we'll see how well you trivia veterans have been paying attention to the answers from previous chapters. Pass this test and face the next real challenge—the Stanley Cup chapter. But don't get caught thinking ahead, that rookie might just sneak one by unexpectedly. *(Answers are on page 111)*

9.1 **Andy Bathgate never won a Stanley Cup.** *True or False?*

9.2 **No clubs from the six-team era ever reached the 100-point mark during the regular season.** *True or False?*

9.3 **Gordie Howe is the only player to score 1,000 points during the six-team era.** *True or False?*

9.4 **The centre ice redline was always checkered (as opposed to one solid red stripe).** *True or False?*

9.5 No defenseman broke Babe Pratt's regular-season points record (set in 1943–44) until Bobby Orr did it after the six-team era. *True or False?*

9.6 Maurice Richard never saw a game at the Montreal Forum before he played there as a Canadiens rookie. *True or False?*

9.7 Longtime Blackhawk goalie Glenn Hall started his NHL career with the Boston Bruins. *True or False?*

9.8 Bill Mosienko's record for the NHL's fastest hat trick (in 21 seconds) was scored while both teams were at full strength. *True or False?*

9.9 Stan Mikita was the only Original Six player to win the NHL scoring race and earn at least 100 penalty minutes. *True or False?*

9.10 Maurice Richard never won an NHL scoring race. *True or False?*

9.11 Maple Leaf Gardens was built during the six-team era. *True or False?*

9.12 Gordie Howe tied and broke Maurice Richard's career mark of 544 goals against the Rocket's old team, the Montreal Canadiens. *True or False?*

9.13 Toronto wore a new Maple Leafs logo on its uniforms for the 1967 Stanley Cup playoffs. *True or False?*

9.14 Norm Ullman never won a Stanley Cup. *True or False?*

9.15 Maurice Richard is the only Original Six player to reach the 500-goal mark. *True or False?*

9.16 The only team to sweep the playoffs in eight straight during the six-team era was the 1952 champion Detroit Red Wings. *True or False?*

9.17 Howie Meeker beat Gordie Howe to win the Calder Trophy as the NHL's top rookie in 1947. *True or False?*

9.18 In 1961, the largest fine in NHL history to date was handed out to a coach. *True or False?*

9.19 Red Kelly won the Lady Byng Trophy (most gentlemanly player) as a Toronto forward, but never while playing defense in Detroit. *True or False?*

9.20 Gordie Howe holds the Original Six record for longest consecutive point-scoring streak in one season. *True or False?*

9.21 Glenn Hall won the Vezina Trophy as top goalie in 1959–60, yet led the league in losses. *True or False?*

9.22 Bobby Hull never played a single game in the minors. *True or False?*

9.23 Six players in the six-team era logged five-goal games. They all played for the Montreal Canadiens. *True or False?*

9.24 No Toronto Maple Leaf ever won the NHL scoring race during the six-team era. *True or False?*

9.25 Terry Sawchuk registered all of his 103 career shutouts during the six-team era. *True or False?*

9.26 Chicago never won a regular-season championship during the six-team era. *True or False?*

9.27   The first arena to separate the penalty box—one for penalized players from the home team and another for visiting teams—was Maple Leaf Gardens. *True or False?*

9.28   The NHL record for most season losses during the six-team era belonged to a team that was backstopped by the league's MVP that same year. *True or False?*

9.29   Phil Esposito was the only 100-point man during the six-team era. *True or False?*

9.30   Maurice Richard was the only Original Six player to reach the 50-goal plateau in one season? *True or False?*

9.31   In 1947, the NHL initiated a rule whereby a scoring player must skate 30 feet with raised arm and stick to signal a goal. That little-known rule is still in the NHL's official rule book. *True or False?*

TRUE OR FALSE?

9.1   False

Bathgate played just 22 playoff games in 11 seasons with New York before being traded to Toronto on February 22, 1964. Two months later, he was tasting Stanley Cup champagne after scoring the Leafs' Cup-clinching goal in game seven of the Toronto-Detroit finals. It was Bathgate's only playoff championship in his 17-year NHL career.

9.2   False

Two clubs on three occasions had +100-point seasons. The 1950–51 Detroit Red Wings registered 101 points on a 44W–13L–13T record; the 1951–52 Wings, 100 points, 44W–14L–12T; and the 1955–56 Montreal Canadiens, 100 points, 45W–15L–10T. All were in 70-game schedules.

9.3   True

Howe hit his historic point number 1,000 with an assist on November 27, 1960. Jean Béliveau was the second NHLer to reach the mark, notching his 1,000th on March 3, 1968, the first year of expansion.

9.4   False

For many years the redline was solid red, until the late-1950s when the league checkered it to distinguish the red and blue rink lines for black-and-white television.

9.5   False

In 1964–65, defenseman Pierre Pilote scored 59 points (14G–45A) to break Babe Pratt's 21-year-old mark of 57 points, set in 1943–44. Pilote's record was in turn wiped out when Orr earned 64 points in 1968–69.

9.6 True

Although Richard listened religiously to "La Soiree du Hockey au Canada" ("Hockey Night in Canada") each Saturday evening on the radio when he was a boy, it wasn't until he graduated to the big club in 1942 that he saw in person the hallowed Montreal Forum.

9.7 False

Hall played four seasons with the Detroit Red Wings, winning the Calder Trophy in 1956 before being traded the following season to Chicago, where he enjoyed a Hall of Fame career for 10 years.

9.8 True

Mosienko scored his 21-second hat trick while both Chicago and New York were at full strength. In fact, the memorable game, on March 23, 1952, was played without penalty.

9.9 False

In the days before team enforcers, players, whatever their status, fended for themselves most nights. Among the 12 scoring leaders of the six-team era, four cooled off in the box for +100 minutes on six occasions. (Dubious mention to Maurice Richard, who missed the scoring crown by one point in 1954–55 while logging 125 penalty minutes.)

The Original Six Point Leaders with 100 Penalty Minutes

Year	Player	GP	G	A	PTS	PIM
1949–50	T. Lindsay	69	23	55	78	141
1953–54	G. Howe	70	33	48	81	109
1955–56	J. Béliveau	70	47	41	88	143
1962–63	G. Howe	70	38	48	86	100
1963–64	S. Mikita	70	39	50	89	146
1964–65	S. Mikita	70	28	59	87	154

9.10 **True**

The closest the Rocket ever came to winning an Art Ross Trophy was in 1955, when he finished one point back of his Canadiens teammate Bernie Geoffrion, 75 to 74 points.

9.11 **False**

The Gardens was built in 1931 at the height of the Depression by the indomitable Conn Smythe, the driving force behind the Leafs for almost half a century.

9.12 **True**

Howe took over the NHL's all-time scoring lead from Richard by netting two goals (the equalizer and the record breaker) two weeks (five games) apart against the Rocket's old team, the Canadiens. The eventful night came in November 1963 as Howe snapped his 545th on a wrist shot past Charlie Hodge.

9.13 **True**

To celebrate Canada's centennial and the start of the Stanley Cup playoffs, Toronto modernized the 35-point Leaf crest and replaced it with an 11-point leaf to resemble the new Canadian flag. The old-style 35-point leaf can still be seen on Toronto's modern-day uniform—as a shoulder patch—in honour of the Leaf teams of the six-team era.

9.14 **True**

Ullman is the Johnny-come-lately of the Stanley Cup. He missed with the Wings in his NHL debut in 1956, a year after Detroit's silverware splurge of four Cups in six years. Then, after labouring for 12 seasons in Detroit as an All-Star centre, and reaching the finals an agonizing five times only to come away empty-handed, he was traded to Toronto in 1967, just months after the Leafs won their fourth (and last) championship. Following eight Cup-less Toronto seasons, Ullman showed up too early on his last pro team: the Gretzky-less WHA Edmonton Oilers.

9.15 **False**

The Rocket was not the only 500-goal man between 1942 and 1967. Five seasons after Richard established the mark on October 19, 1957, against Glenn Hall, Gordie Howe pegged his 500th on March 14, 1962 (against Gump Worsley). The Rocket netted 500 goals in 863 games; Mr. Hockey in 1,045 matches.

9.16 **False**

It was only done twice, first by the Red Wings in 1952 against Toronto and Montreal in an eight-game post-season brooming, and then by the 1960 Montreal Canadiens. After disposing of Chicago in four straight (two by shutouts), the Habs allowed Toronto just five goals in the final series sweep to win an unprecedented fifth consecutive Stanley Cup. Jacques Plante was the first goalie to wear a mask in post-season and 38-year-old Rocket Richard played his last game, scoring his 34th career goal of the finals (82nd in total playoff action), still an NHL record.

9.17 **True**

Howe's first season totals (7–15–22 in 58 games) did not excite Calder voters, who awarded Meeker top rookie honours after he posted an impressive 27–18–45 record in 55 games with Toronto. Meeker played another seven NHL seasons, never equalling his rookie year's point output.

9.18 **True**

Canadiens coach Toe Blake was fined an astronomical $2,000 for decking referee Dalton McArthur during the 1961 playoffs. No individual had ever received such a hefty fine.

9.19 **False**

Kelly's 1961 Lady Byng with the Maple Leafs was not his first but his fourth turn-the-other-cheek award, having been honoured on three previous occasions (1951, 1953 and 1954) as a Red Wing defenseman.

9.20 False

Boston's Bronco Horvath holds the record, scoring 16 goals and 17 assists in 22 consecutive games in 1959–60.

9.21 False

Hall battled Jacques Plante head-to-head in the Vezina race all season, only to lose in the final game after giving up five goals in a 5–5 Boston tie. Hall, who led the league in losses, missed clinching the Vezina by two goals, or a goals-against average of 2.57 compared to Plante's 2.54. (At that time, goalies were awarded the Vezina based on the lowest averages.)

9.22 True

Hull's 1957 debut at the Hawks training camp was so impressive that he jumped straight to the big club, never playing a game in the minor leagues.

9.23 False

Toronto's Howie Meeker and Syd Howe of Detroit were the only non-Canadiens players to produce five-goal games during the six-team era. The successful Habs were Ray Getliffe, Maurice Richard, Bernie Geoffrion and Bobby Rousseau.

9.24 True

Never mind the six-team era, the NHL hasn't seen a league scoring champ from Toronto since Gordie Drillon in 1938.

9.25 False

Sawchuk's 103 shutouts are an NHL record, and all but three of them were posted before expansion in 1967.

9.26 False

The Blackhawks' 40-year wait to win a regular-season championship ended the last season of the six-team era, 1966–67, when Chicago finished with 94 points, 17 points ahead of second-place Montreal.

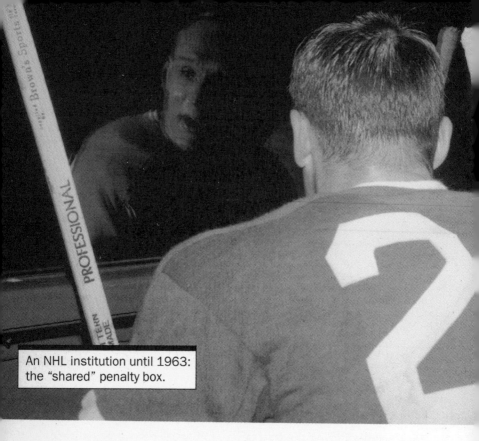

An NHL institution until 1963: the "shared" penalty box.

9.27 True

Maple Leaf Gardens was the first NHL arena to provide separate home and visitor penalty boxes. The 1963 move was long overdue, considering the altercations that resulted when combatants sat within striking distance of each other. Here, Frank Mahovlich discusses the finer points of clutch-and-grab hockey, only inches from his Boston counterpart.

9.28 True

Despite Chicago's abysmal 1953–54 record (12–51–7), goalie Al Rollins (12–47–7) picked up the Hart as league MVP.

9.29 False

Esposito was the NHL's first 100-point man, but he didn't notch it until after league expansion, on March 2, 1969.

9.30 False

Richard achieved hockey's ultimate scoring record first, but he was not the only Original Six 50-goal man. Bernie Geoffrion wired his 50th in 1961; Bobby Hull did it three times during the six-team era, in 1962, 1966 and 1967, and again in 1969 and 1972.

9.31 False

Although players had long celebrated a goal by raising their stick, in 1947 the NHL began enforcing the custom in order to more readily identify the scorer. Under the policy, the Canadiens' Billy Reay was the first. Later, in the same game, Toe Blake scored, but forgot to raise his arms, and then Chicago's Roy Conacher did do it, only to have his goal called back. No wonder there is no such NHL rule in the books today.

BABE, BUTCH AND THE GUMPER

Some of hockey's best nicknames have been inspired by the players of the six-team era. In this game, match the following 25 nicknames with the players who proudly earned them. If you've forgotten any names, we make references throughout the book.

(Solutions are on page 134)

Golden Jet	Flash	Babe	The Cat	Moose
Mr. Hockey	Butch	Ironman	Muzz	Black Jack
Leapin'	Dit	Ulcers	Rocket	Teeder
Apple Cheeks	Tough	Bronco	King	Terrible
Boom-Boom	Sugar	Toe	Turk	China Wall

Walter "_____" Pratt

Frank "_____" Hollett

"_____ _____" Gordie Howe

Joseph "_____" Horvath

Ted "_____" Kennedy

Emile "_____" Bouchard

Murray "_____" Patrick

Hector "_____" Blake

"_____Ted" Lindsay

Elmer "_____" Vasko

Walter "_____" Broda

"_____Tony" Leswick

Bernie "_____ - _____" Geoffrion

"_____ Jim" Henry

"_____ Lou" Fontinato

Francis "_____" Clancy

Frank "_____" McCool

"_____ _____" Bobby Hull

Aubrey "_____" Clapper

Lorne "_____" Worsley

Harry "_____ _____" Lumley

Emile "_____ _____" Francis

Johnny Bower, "_____ _____"

Maurice "_____" Richard

Johnny "_____" Wilson

Chapter TEN

SILVER DYNASTY

NO HOCKEY DYNASTIES HAVE dominated the playoffs more completely than the Stanley Cup-winning Maple Leafs, Red Wings and Canadiens of the six-team era. Except for Chicago's lone championship, the Original Six era was characterized by unparalled disparity. The first club to win three successive Cups (Toronto's 1947–48–49 champions) came from this period. In five straight seasons, Detroit claimed four playoff championships. But no NHL club, before or since, has been able to equal the five Cups strung together by Montreal from 1956 to 1960. It's been said that the Canadiens' third forward line was better than most first lines on other teams. In this final chapter, we go to the dance, dressed to dominate.

(Answers are on page 123)

10.1 **Why do Detroit fans throw octopi on the ice during the playoffs?**

    A. The octopus, with its sucker-lined tentacles, is tossed at slimy on-ice officials after a bad call

    B. In memory of Wings goalie Terry Sawchuk, whose legs and arms were likened to those of an octopus

    C. The eight-legged octopus represents a playoff sweep

    D. The octopus, a cephalopod native to Lake Michigan, is in-season during the playoffs

10.2 **Which position in the regular-season final standings has most often seen its team win the Stanley Cup?**
A. First place
B. Second place
C. Third place
D. Fourth place

10.3 **What playoff format in the semi-final round determined Stanley Cup finalists?**
A. First place vs. second place; third vs. fourth
B. First place vs. third place; second vs. fourth
C. First place vs. fourth place; second vs. third
D. Second place vs. third place; fourth place eliminated

10.4 **Which Original Six skater played in the most playoff games?**
A. Gordie Howe
B. Henri Richard
C. Marcel Pronovost
D. Red Kelly

10.5 **How many times in the 25 Stanley Cups of the six-team era were the finals played between two American teams?**
A. Never
B. Three times
C. Six times
D. Nine times

10.6 **Which Stanley Cup-losing coach said: "If I had shaken hands, I wouldn't have meant it, and I refuse to be a hypocrite."**
A. The Maple Leafs' Punch Imlach
B. The Blackhawks' Billy Reay
C. The Canadiens' Dick Irvin
D. The Bruins' Milt Schmidt

10.7 Which NHL tough guy scored a Stanley Cup-winning goal during the six-team era?

A. Eddie Shack

B. Ted Green

C. John Ferguson

D. Elmer "Moose" Vasko

10.8 In what Toronto-Montreal Stanley Cup final series did every game go into overtime?

A. The 1947 Stanley Cup finals

B. The 1951 Stanley Cup finals

C. The 1960 Stanley Cup finals

D. The 1967 Stanley Cup finals

10.9 In what Original Six year did the Chicago Blackhawks win the Stanley Cup?

A. 1960

B. 1961

C. 1962

D. 1963

10.10 Name the first team in NHL history to win three consecutive Stanley Cup championships. (And the seasons they set the mark.)

A. The Detroit Red Wings

B. The Montreal Canadiens

C. The Toronto Maple Leafs

D. The Boston Bruins

10.11 Which Original Six team lost the most Stanley Cup finals?

A. The Montreal Canadiens

B. The Detroit Red Wings

C. The Boston Bruins

D. The Toronto Maple Leafs

10.12 **How many U.S.-born players appeared on a Stanley Cup-winning team during the six-team era?**

A. One

B. Between two and five

C. Between six and 10

D. At least 11

10.13 **Who was the NHL's inaugural winner of the Conn Smythe Trophy as playoff MVP?**

A. Glenn Hall

B. Dave Keon

C. Jean Béliveau

D. Stan Mikita

10.14 **Which Stanley Cup-winning coach inspired his team by saying: "For some of you it's a farewell. Go out there and put that puck down their throats."?**

A. Detroit's Sid Abel

B. Chicago's Rudy Pilous

C. Montreal's Dick Irvin

D. Toronto's Punch Imlach

SILVER DYNASTY

C. The eight-legged octopus represents a playoff sweep
The throwing of octopi was a Red Wings tradition that started during the 1952 finals between Montreal and Detroit. Fans at the Olympia began tossing the eight-legged creatures onto the ice to represent the eight games Detroit needed to sweep the two-round playoffs that year. The Red Wings never repeated the feat in their two subsequent successful trips to the championships (1954 and 1955), but the octopus gimmick caught on and continues today, despite the impossibility of an eight-game sweep in the post-expansion four-round playoff format.

10.2 **A. First place**
Winning the NHL regular-season championship is a good (but not great) barometer of who will win the Stanley Cup. Nothing new there, since first-place teams captured the Cup 14 times (or 57 per cent of the time) in 25 post-seasons during the six-team era. Second-, third- and fourth-place finishers tallied six, four and one Cup respectively. Interestingly, each time Detroit won the Cup they finished in first place. The Canadiens won seven Cups after 12 first-place finishes. Inversely, the least predictable team was Toronto, who won seven of their nine Cups after recording a second-, third-, and even one fourth-place finish in the standings. This means the Leafs won two Cups while finishing first, Toronto's only first-place finishes in 25 seasons.

10.3 **B. First place vs. third place; second vs. fourth**
Only one playoff format was used throughout the six-team era. The top four clubs played each other in a best-of-seven semi-final round that pitted the first-place team

against the third-place finisher. The club in second place challenged the fourth-place team. The winners of the two semi-finals then went dancing in a best-of-seven Stanley Cup final.

10.4   D. Red Kelly

After winning four Stanley Cups with Detroit in the 1950s, Kelly was traded to Toronto, where he won another four championships and amassed a record 164 playoff games between 1947–48 through 1966–67, besting Howe (150) and Pronovost (134).

10.5   B. Three times

During the six-team era there were only three all-American Stanley Cup finals. Two were won by Detroit, against Boston (1943) and New York (1950), and the third Cup was won by Chicago, versus Detroit (1961). Toronto and Montreal played five all-Canadian finals, the Leafs edging the Canadiens 3–2 in championships.

10.6   C. The Canadiens' Dick Irvin

The most bitter rivalry in hockey during the 1950s was between the league's two powerhouses, the Red Wings and Canadiens. So intense was their mutual dislike, that when sharing trains between back-to-back games they refused to acknowledge one another as they made their way to the dining car. Fights even broke out on occasion. The Montreal–Detroit battles were most fierce in the playoffs, particularly between 1952 and 1956. During those five years, four Stanley Cup finals were played out at the Olympia and the Forum, two series going the maximum seven games. Game seven of the 1954 showdown was a classic. The largest crowd in Detroit history witnessed a seesaw clash that went deadlocked 1–1 into overtime, thanks to brilliant goaltending by Terry Sawchuk and Gerry McNeil. But a fluke goal by Tony Leswick ended the thriller. It came on a shift change as Leswick flipped the puck at the Montreal net. Doug Harvey reached for it, but the puck bounced off his glove and behind McNeil to score. The Olympia shook and the shocked Canadiens stormed off the ice without congratulating their victorious rivals. Later, a disheartened Irvin could only say he would be a hypocrite for shaking hands.

10.7 A. Eddie Shack

Shack classed himself with the likes of Howe, Béliveau and Richard at least once. The biggest goal of his 17-year career came on April 18, 1963, when he placed himself among this elite group by scoring a Stanley Cup winner. Jostling for position in front of the Wings net, Shack somehow managed to tip a shot rifled from the blueline by Toronto rookie defenseman Kent Douglas. The rubber danced past a startled Terry Sawchuk, giving the Leafs a 2–1 lead with 6:32 remaining in the game. Ahead in the series 3–1 in games, Toronto won the finale 3–1 and Shack became the improbable hero as the Leafs captured their 9th Stanley Cup. Shack scored just six goals in 74 post-season games.

10.8 B. The 1951 Stanley Cup finals

Although Toronto defeated the Canadiens, winning the best-of-seven series 4–1, Montreal could only be subdued in each loss in overtime. Five different sharpshooters tallied the winners. All four Leafs notched the only OT goals of their careers, while Montreal's Rocket Richard registered his fourth of a career-record six overtime goals. The 1951 final series is the only Stanley Cup in NHL history in which every game went into overtime.

The 1951 Stanley Cup Finals • Overtime Results

Date	Score	OT/Time	Winner
Apr. 11	Toronto 3, Montreal 2	5:51	Sid Smith
Apr. 14	Montreal 3, Toronto 2	2:55	Maurice Richard
Apr. 17	Toronto 2, Montreal 1	4:47	Ted Kennedy
Apr. 19	Toronto 3, Montreal 2	5:15	Harry Watson
Apr. 21	Toronto 3, Montreal 2	2:53	Bill Barilko

10.9 B. 1961

In more than a half-century, Chicago has managed only one Stanley Cup, in 1961. The all-American final between the Hawks and Detroit went six games and featured head-to-head firepower from Gordie Howe and Bobby Hull, the leading scorers of post-season. If hockey fever hit Chicago hard, there was good reason. Since their last Cup 23 years earlier (1938), the Hawks had missed the playoffs a record 14 times and the franchise might have collapsed, except for an intervention by the league that moved players from other NHL clubs to Chicago for a rebuilding program. It worked. Players such as captain Ed Litzenberger (from Montreal) filled out the team, which also featured some homegrown talent, including Hull, Stan Mikita and Pierre Pilote.

10.10 C. The Toronto Maple Leafs

The real story of the NHL's first three-time Stanley Cup-winner is the rebuilding job Conn Smythe and Hap Day performed after the Leafs failed to make the playoffs in 1946. And they did it almost overnight, starting on defense by recruiting big, tough talented rookies, such as Garth Boesch, Gus Mortson, Jim Thomson and Bill Barilko. On offense, rookie-of-the-year Howie Meeker joined eight holdovers—Syl Apps, Ted Kennedy, Turk Broda, Don and Nick Metz, Bill Ezinicki, Gaye Stewart and Wally Stanowski—to form the nucleus of the Leafs' 1947 champions. Not satisfied, Smythe then engineered hockey's biggest trade up to that time, dealing five Leafs to Chicago for ace centre Max Bentley. Toronto now had Apps, Kennedy and Bentley, three of the top six centres in the game and enough firepower to drive three solid lines. They cruised through the 1948 playoffs, crushing the Wings in the Cup finals four straight, and repeated the deed in 1949, victimizing Detroit and Howe's mighty Production Line. On their path to history the Leafs dominated three successive Cup final series by winning 12 of 14 games, with nine straight victories.

10.11 B. The Detroit Red Wings

The Wings were the perennial bridesmaids of the Cup finals during the six-team era. They dressed for the big dance 13 times in 25 seasons, winning five Cups but dropping eight other championships. Detroit's nemesis was the Maple Leafs, who brought down the Wings on five occasions: 1945, 1948, 1949, 1963 and 1964.

10.12 A. One

It's amazing that during the 25 seasons of the six-team era only one U.S.-born player won the Stanley Cup. His name is Wayne Hicks, a right winger from Aberdeen, Washington, whose family moved to Saskatchewan when he was just one year old. In 1951, at age 14, Hicks was signed by Chicago and played for the next 10 years in their farm system, until that fateful night, April 18, 1961. The Hawks' Murray Balfour had broken his arm in game five and Hicks was called up to replace the star forward in what would be the Cup-winning game. Chicago beat Detroit 5–1 (and won the series, 4–2) and Hicks got his chance at immortality. As he says, "Hey, they didn't put me on the power play or to kill penalties, but I did play on the same line with Bobby Hull and Bill Hay." Today, on Hicks's mantlepiece rests his miniature Stanley Cup, the only one belonging to an American from the Original Six era. (The last American Cup winner before Hicks was Eveleth, Minnesota-native, Frank Brimsek, who won with Boston in 1941. The next after Hicks was Bobby Sheehan of Weymouth, Massachusetts, who played on the champion Canadiens in 1971.)

10.13 C. Jean Béliveau

It was a seismic Stanley Cup final. Characterized by frayed nerves and featuring two explosive, equally-matched teams, it culminated in a seventh and deciding game at the Montreal Forum. On one side were the Chicago superstars, Bobby Hull, Stan Mikita and Glenn Hall; on the other, Cup veterans Béliveau, Henri Richard and

Dick Duff. Just 14 seconds into the crucial game, Béliveau scored on Hall. Five minutes later he deked out Chicago's defense and passed to Duff for another. Coach Toe Blake said Béliveau had never enjoyed a series like it. The Habs won 4–0 and captain Béliveau, with eight goals and eight assists in 13 playoff games, was voted the first winner of the Conn Smythe Trophy for his sterling play-off performance.

10.14 D. Toronto's Punch Imlach

It's been called the miracle Stanley Cup, and for many, Imlach's "Over-The-Hill Gang" of 1967 performed the supernatural. With seven players over 36 years old, an average team age of 31, and "youngsters" like 27-year-old Dave Keon, the Leafs stormed past first-place Chicago, winning the semi-finals 4–2 before challenging the favoured Canadiens. Stanley Cup fever was red-hot as Canada's arch-rivals squared off amid the 1967 Centennial celebrations. Montreal had Expo 67; Toronto sported a new stylized Maple Leaf logo resembling the new Canadian flag. The aging Leafs played brilliantly, particularly veteran netminders Johnny Bower and Terry Sawchuk. Before game six, with the Leafs ahead 3–2 in the series, Imlach delivered his "farewell" line. It struck a chord for 37-year-old Sawchuk, who stopped 46 shots and helped the Leafs "put the puck down their throats," defeating Jean Béliveau's Canadiens and claiming Toronto's 11th Stanley Cup.

Four-time Stanley Cup-winner **Johnny Bower** wearing the Leafs' classic "Original Six" jersey.

GAME 1: THE PINWHEEL PUCK

GAME 2: THE RECORD HOLDERS

1. Bobby Hull
2. Stan Mikita
3. Andy Bathgate
4. Glenn Hall
5. Maurice Richard
6. Gordie Howe
7. Jerry Toppazzini
8. Bill Durnan
9. Bernie Geoffrion
10. Terry Sawchuk
11. Syd Howe
12. Gus Bodnar
13. Jean Béliveau
14. Harry Lumley
15. Howie Meeker

GAME 3: HOCKEY CROSSWORD

GAME 4: THE AMAZING DOZEN

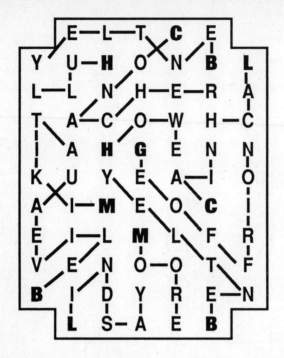

GAME 5: THE GORDIE HOWE
NUMBERS GAME

1. 21 regular seasons in six-team era
2. 156 points in playoffs
3. 49 goals in a season
4. Eleven 30-or-more-goal seasons
5. 825 assists
6. 1,501 points
7. Nine seconds, fastest goal

8. 109 penalty minutes
9. Four 40-or-more-goal seasons
10. 1,398 games
11. 91 assists in playoffs
12. 12 points in finals
13. 649 goals
14. Eighteen 20-or-more-goal seasons
15. Eight goals in semi-finals

GAME 6: STANLEY CUP HEROES

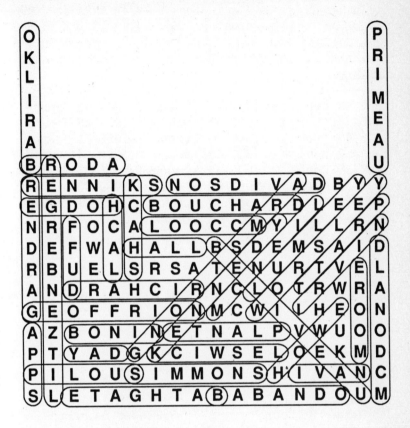

The remaining letters spell out in descending order: B-O-W-E-R and S-A-W-C-H-U-K, the tandem goaltending unit that shut the door on the Canadiens.

GAME 7: LISTEN UP!

1. Olympia PA Announcer (1950s)
2. Turk Broda (1940s)
3. Bep Guidolin (1942)
4. Phil Esposito (1967)
5. Glenn Hall (1961)
6. Maurice Richard (1963)
7. Ted Lindsay (1950s)
8. Conn Smythe (1957)

GAME 8: THE CUP WINNERS

The Canadiens won the Cup 10 times (five-in-a-row between 1956 and 1960); the Maple Leafs, no slouches either, took it on nine occasions; the Red Wings captured five championships; the Blackhawks just one, and the Bruins and Rangers drew blanks in their finals.

1942–43	Detroit	1943–44	Montreal	1944–45	Toronto
1945–46	Montreal	1946–47	Toronto	1947–48	Toronto
1948–49	Toronto	1949–50	Detroit	1950–51	Toronto
1951–52	Detroit	1952–53	Toronto	1953–54	Detroit
1954–55	Detroit	1955–56	Montreal	1956–57	Montreal
1957–58	Montreal	1958–59	Montreal	1959–60	Montreal
1960–61	Chicago	1961–62	Toronto	1962–63	Toronto
1963–64	Toronto	1964–65	Montreal	1965–66	Montreal
1966–67	Toronto				

GAME 9: BABE, BUTCH AND THE GUMPER

Walter "**Babe**" Pratt

Frank "**Flash**" Hollett

"**Mr. Hockey**" Gordie Howe

Joseph "**Bronco**" Horvath

Ted "**Teeder**" Kennedy

Emile "**Butch**" Bouchard

Murray "**Muzz**" Patrick

Hector "**Toe**" Blake

"**Terrible Ted**" Lindsay

Elmer "**Moose**" Vasko

Walter "**Turk**" Broda

"**Tough Tony**" Leswick

Bernie "**Boom-Boom**" Geoffrion

"**Sugar Jim**" Henry

"**Leapin' Lou**" Fontinato

Francis "**King**" Clancy

Frank "**Ulcers**" McCool

"**Golden Jet**" Bobby Hull

Aubrey "**Dit**" Clapper

Lorne "**Gump**" Worsley

Harry "**Apple Cheeks**" Lumley

Emile "**The Cat**" Francis

Johnny Bower, "**China Wall**"

Maurice "**Rocket**" Richard

Johnny "**Ironman**" Wilson

ACKNOWLEDGEMENTS

Care has been taken to trace ownership of copyright material contained in this book. The publishers welcome any information that will enable them to rectify any reference or provide credit in subsequent editions.

The author gratefully acknowledges the help of Phil Pritchard at the Hockey Hall of Fame; Ron Reusch of CFCF–12 in Montreal; Wayne Hicks; Ginette Barts of the *Detroit News;* Robert Clements at Greystone Books; a number of hockey writers and broadcasters, who helped make this book possible through their own efforts during the six-team era; as well as fact checker Allen Bishop, graphic artist Ivor Tiltin and puzzle designer Adrien van Vlaardingen.

PHOTO CREDITS

David Bier: page 24

The Detroit News: page 67

Graphic Artists/Hockey Hall of Fame archives: page 5

Hockey Hall of Fame archives: pages 8, 27, 45, 53, 60, 73, 93, 99, 104, 129

Imperial Oil–Turofsky/Hockey Hall of Fame archives: pages 10, 15, 37, 48, 78–79, 83, 88, 110, 116–117, 122

The Montreal Star: page 33

Frank Prasak/Hockey Hall of Fame archives: pages 35, 135

SELECTED BIBLIOGRAPHY

Coleman, Charles L. *The Trail of the Stanley Cup.* 3 vols. Montreal: National Hockey League, 1976.

Diamond, Dan. *Years of Glory, The Six-Team Era.* Toronto: McClelland & Stewart, 1994.

Fischler, Stan and Shirley, and Hughes, Morgan, and Romain, Joseph, and Duplacey, James. *20th Century Hockey Chronicle.* Lincolnwood, Illinois: Publications International, 1994.

Goyens, Chrys, and Turowetz, Allan. *Lions in Winter.* Toronto: McGraw-Hill Ryerson, 1994.

Hollander, Zander. *The Complete Encyclopedia of Hockey.* Detroit: Visable Ink Press, 1993.

Houston, William. *Maple Leaf Blues.* Toronto: McClelland & Stewart, 1990.

Hunter, Douglas. *Open Ice, The Tim Hunter Story.* Toronto: Viking, 1994.

Kendall, Brian. *100 Great Moments in Hockey.* Toronto: Viking, 1994.

Leonetti, Mike. *Hockey's Golden Era.* Toronto: Macmillan of Canada, 1993.

McKinley, Michael. *Hockey Hall of Fame Legends.* Toronto: Viking, 1993.

ABOUT THE AUTHOR

Don Weekes saw his first NHL game at the Montreal
Forum in 1958. He is currently writing and producing a
television documentary on the Canadiens' new 21,000-
seat Forum, scheduled to open in 1996. He also produces
hockey segments for the nationally syndicated television
sports magazine, "Hockey World."